LALITAMBA

Issue 4

Cover art by Susanne von Schroeder.

Printed in accordance with
the Sustainable Forestry Initiative.

ISBN 978-09778633-3-4
ISSN 1930-0662

The name for the journal was inspired by a devotional song, "Lalitamba, Lalitamba," sung on a tour through India. In early 2004, we traveled through the country in an effort to alleviate the suffering that comes with poverty, illness, and loss of hope. The journal was founded in November of 2004.

The name Lalitamba means Divine Mother. In India, the Divine Mother is thought of as *jagado dharini,* or She who supports the universe. The journal *Lalitamba* publishes writings and artwork that explore meaning, relationship, and truth. It is a journal of modern mysticism.

Submission Guidelines: Please submit up to five poems or one work of prose per envelope. Work should be previously unpublished. Please include SASE and contact information, including email address. Please address all correspondence to:

Lalitamba
P.O. Box 131
Planetarium Station
New York, NY 10024

Subscriptions are $12 for one annual issue, plus $4.50 postage and handling. We are a 501(c)(3) nonprofit organization serving hospitals, prisons, and shelters.

www.lalitamba.com

Lalitamba is affiliated with Refuge, a women's shelter in New York City.

www.threejewelsrefuge.org

TABLE OF CONTENTS

LETTERS AND PRAYERS   11

INTERVIEWS

An Interview with Daniel Ladinsky   126

POETRY

Hearing the Silence   17
Should You Ask Me   28
On the Verge of God   28
For My Friend   29
After Kabir   30
Spirituality Is Nothing More   30
Self-Realizing Creative Love   31
Untitled   31
Sitting at 14th   32
Heaven   32
Maharishi Passed   33
The Empty Hand Holds the World   35
Do I Wake or Sleep   35
After "Buddha's Court"   36
After "The Gospel
According to St. Matthew"   37
Middle East Poets   44
Shadows   45
Meditation   45
Jesus   46
Noah   46
Yasoda Accuses Krishna of Eating Dirt   47
Sri Hanuman Chalisa   51
Cross & Culm   62

Los sueños de la razón   68
The Beauty Queen's Apocalypse   71
The Thousand Names of Bala   86
The Bent: Lily Susses   100
Invitation   116
Where Are You?   117
After Rereading the *Tao Te Ching*   118
Nothing There   119
So That You Can Plant More Wheat   136
The Body Is Like Mary   137
Nothing Like a Yesterday   138
Be Like That Cat   138
Pace   142
asking my grandfather   143
And I Didn't Completely Shut the Car Door 143
happiness forever?   151
Beyond Recognition   156
Blessing of Bees   163
The Angel and the Gargoyle   181
Angry Enough To Die   181
Flying in the Sea   182
Going out of Town   183
Charley Plays a Tune   184
Hiddenbrooke   187
Conundrum   193
A Circle of Stones   194
At the Bakery in Chinatown   194
It Happened   195
Mountains and Pine Forests   195
Meditation at Moose Creek   196
92 Rapple Drive   197
He Said One Memory or Rapple Drive   198

FICTION

In the Dark   19
A Word of Silence   63

The Girl in Pigtails   72
From Gravity We Are Free   114
Rebirthing Without Having To Die   141
My Last Gift   185
A Journey, a Reckoning, and a Miracle   199

ESSAYS

They Witnessed the Light   39
The Balance of Compassion   120
Marriage of Half-Empty to Half-Full   145
The Sacred and the Mundane   152
Emptiness   155
Life in the Round   157
Entanglement   165
Water Burn   178

ART

Water Lily   49
Untitled Drawing   69
Acoma Pueblo   139
Stepped Pyramid   189
Light with Columns   191

CONTRIBUTORS' NOTES   205

LETTERS AND PRAYERS

Tonight, instead of trying to talk to You in my bed,
I talk to You with my pen. I write a Psalm, perhaps.
I ask for what I ask for every night:
      Heal my heart, and let me not be crazy,
      and give me strength to live a good life.

Like on other nights, I do not know if You are there.
I do not know if You hear me.
It has been said by sages that You talk to men.
I have not heard Your voice, I do not think,
but yet...I know there is a You
by what You have made:
by the stars and the grasses in the marshes,
by how You grow flowers and trees
and how they breathe,
by how Your perfumes fill the woods
and by the more than myriads of intricacies
Your hand has crafted.
Maybe then, for me in some small way,
we have heard each other.
If this is so, I cannot say.
And now I end this with the end
of the Bedtime Shema:
      Stand in awe and sin not.
      Commune with your own heart
      upon your bed and be still.
      Selah

Marvin Blaustein
Brooklyn, NY

A Father's Lament—

You know I'm a lousy sinner
dressed up in good deeds
just to live with myself.
Sure, I say grace before dinner,
make it to church most Sundays,
try to plant the seed
of your love in my kids,
but failed there, it appears.
A scar in my heart bleeds
slowly
because I can't explain what I did
or didn't do to lose them.
Maybe in the fullness of time,
they'll come to you as their lives skid
close to the darkness
that calls and condemns
us all.
Maybe not. Like most of what I pray for,
the pebble into a gem,
the lost into a found,
to stand upright after I fall,
I'll keep at it with faith.
I kneel before you—naked,
blindfolded, praying against the wall:
open their hearts, Lord, and keep them safe.

David James
Linden, MI

Beloved,

Crossing the Gobi turned out to be
nowhere near as hard as we had imagined it.
We moved stealthily and steadily into the desert
hundreds of yards above pre-sand Egypt.
For navigating through the deadly sandstorms
one of our party had come up with the idea
of twelve-foot stilts, which worked admirably.
During the maelstroms, although we could not see
the dunes playing pranks beneath our feet, we were
able to find our footing by watching the contours
of the whirling sands around our heads, and at times,
when we stuck our necks out, we could see a few feet
ahead — at times we could almost glimpse
the shrouds of light from the sun.
Alas, one dark beam did pierce my heart —
Soloviev, whom I had cured of his
vodka addiction, and whom I had come to love
like a brother, wandered off to find water
during the whirling darkness at midday
and was bitten through the neck by a wild camel.
We found him with his wide eyes still open.
But *Forward, march!* — We are finding the imperative
trackings of hidden cartographers,
and far ahead the slashing clear skies
of gigantic mountains are visible. We have
but to approach them and pass over.

Michael Creedon
Oakland, CA

The journal is an offering
for the liberation of all beings.

Brian Cronwall

HEARING THE SILENCE

Outside the window, silent night-wind,
ready to gust, is like a colt
hearing the stable-gate open.

Palm fronds brush green, their
percussive voices telling stories,
not lies. One set of tires

shushes wet pavement. Another's
gentle hiss-roll is a parting of wet night
to make room for a dog-bark,

a gecko's shattering laughter,
a bird's two notes. I'm unable
to name the tune. How the breath

responds, quiet until listened to,
gentle as pine needles falling
in light rain, sure as breakers embracing

distant darker sands. My heart
and watch are synchronous and strong.
They pulse like stars, stream-water, a pen-point

flowing onto the page, sitting there,
perhaps forever, a window remaining
open. The night begins to sing,

or is it me? A hiccup in the air
like jade dropped into a sink
full of water, dripping long

into the pregnant darkness, learning
to become a chord. I am a cloud-called
window tonight, screened and open,
hearing the silence begin to erupt.

Edward Black

In the Dark

Night. No moon and dark. Untended, unkempt, the weeds taking over. Make out the lines of the slanted roof. Now, follow the footpath inside. There they lie. An old man and woman asleep on the *tatami* floor. A deep, uneasy sleep. A toss then a turn. A mumble and a groan.

Now, move in closer. See her rest the back of her hand to her forehead.

Listen.

She speaks: "I remember. The atomic bomb struck. There was a loud, blinding flash. How the skies darkened, and a black rain fell. How the clouds lifted, and burnt bodies appeared strewn about the streets we searched. The arms and legs dangled from the scorched trees. My sister and I found our parents in a gutter, charred and blistered, hollow sockets for eyes and holes for ears, their mouths stretched open, unable to cry out our names any longer. And how we ran."

Her old voice fades.

But look. Her husband beside her now stirs: "I was captured, along with three other American soldiers. The Japanese bound our wrists. With their bayonets pricking our backs, they marched us into the roadside jungle to kill us. Our fears mounted with every step. Then, one by one, they blindfolded each soldier and asked if he had a last statement to make before they raised their guns and shot him dead. One man wished goodbye to a loved one. Another man cried out to heaven for mercy."

"We ran," she says. "We passed the rubble of our school, ripped-up nuns, and a pile of our classmates' heads. One morning, at the railroad station, a hungry week later, my sister took a last look at me. As the outbound train hurtled by, she threw herself before it onto the tracks."

"When they got to me," he explains, "a Japanese soldier asked if I had any last thing I wished to say. 'Yeah,' I said. 'Don't shoot me.'

"It turned quiet. I smelled gunsmoke. I felt the pocket *Bible* they'd taken put into my hands, as they cut loose the rope. They took off my blindfold. I saw a slight smile on the captain's face, and they let me go."

See his arm now flung across Mutsuko. Look how short she is, for after the bomb she ceased to grow.

How did they meet? No. Don't ask. They cannot hear you.

It was a muggy day, a year after the war was over. Mutsuko was pushing her fruit cart to set up along the Kyobashigawa River and its bridge that hadn't fallen. A jeep of G.I.s splashed by and muddied her. They sped away, honking and trailing laughter.

The next morning, an army chaplain she recognized from the jeep showed up at her cart. In shined shoes and a pressed uniform, he stood before her, as she stood in her washed kimono. He removed his hat — a sign of respect? — then motioned her to place the three peaches he'd purchased into his hat. She was watching him walk off when a motorcade crossed the bridge and ground to a halt. General MacArthur got out.

The chaplain snapped on his hat and bolted to attention. He stood erect in the hot sun, saluting, the crushed peaches leaking down his rigid neck and stern face.

The vehicles gone, he turned and looked back at her in the shade. He shrugged his wet shoulders. They both laughed. It was her first time since the bomb fell.

He received his discharge papers, and they married. They began the work to convert their simple wooden house in Hiroshima into a temple for Jesus.

Roy told Mutsuko it was better that she be the one to tend the yard. "With your stunted growth, you're closer to the ground," he said and laughed. He put up an altar inside and sat on the floor at the desk at the window. Looking out into the yard, an open *Bible* before him, he penned a *senryu*:

To reach up to
heaven she digs down
into the earth.

They worked hard, but few visitors came. Most strolled the grounds and left. At times, one lingered to bend and sniff the flowers, but never to go in to the altar to bow and pray.

Should passersby wander near the window, he ventured out and told them of Jesus. Any initial interest in the story would abruptly wane, however, with his telling of the Resurrection. They'd gaze up at the roof before turning to leave.

"It's no temple," they'd exclaim, passing through the gate. "It's just a house with a nice yard."

"What we need is a bell," Mutsuko said, when she came in one evening.

Roy slid the desk to the middle of the room. Now, it was a dinner table.

"What's a temple without a bell?" she said.

Roy shrugged.

"A house," she said.

He laughed. Then, he said, "Mighty expensive."

She poured the tea, and he took a rice ball.

"We got to eat," he said. "Maybe we could dig up the plants and the flowers, and put in a vegetable garden."

"Whoever heard of a temple with vegetables?" she said.

"It'd have to be a good-sized garden," he said.

After the meal, Roy dragged away the dinner table. "Why can't they just imagine we have a bell?" he said.

"It's not the same," she said, laying out the futon. He returned the table to the window—and it turned back into a writing desk.

Now, hear old Roy as he sleeps in the dark: "Why do we always blow out the candle before our lovemaking. Is it that the dark blots out reality? Is it so we can imagine it to be more than it is?"

Hear the sleeping old Mutsuko: "Is it that the dark unifies everything? In the dark all becomes one. Or is it that the dark makes everything in the room disappear, so that all becomes nothing? In this nothingness, does not everything again become one?"

Lying down together in the dark, the young couple agreed. Without a child, two cannot be a family. Though two can be husband and wife, only a child can turn a husband into a father, the wife into a mother, and make them all a family.

They tried their best. They turned to prayer. Still, Mutsuko stayed barren. As the years went by, her faith wavered. She began to show doubt.

Roy held steadfast.

"You always get something," he informed her of prayer one evening.

"What's that?"

"An answer."

"Well then, apparently the answer is *no*."

"Still, we must do our part," he said. He laughed and blew out the candle.

A minute later the wick was relit. Roy shook out the match. He got up. "No, it's not you," he said. "Too much tea at supper." He headed outside barefoot to pee.

Standing at the *ajisai* bush he looked up into the stars. Then, he looked between his legs at what his hands held. Mutsuko watched him shuffle back and forth, directing the stream of pee, watering the flowerbed.

"That's an odd coupling," she said when he came back. "What's used for passion is also used for pissing."

"A God who's ludicrously practical," he said. "Imagine that."

Years of marriage passed, without a bell, without a child. Roy persevered, reading the *Bible* and writing.

Two halves to
make a whole
can never merge.

Mutsuko hoed the row of squash and potatoes. To offset it, Roy put in a colorful pool of carp to keep the place more temple-like. Still, few visitors came. Then, one night he had a revelation: They should put in an outhouse.

"But nobody's ever here long enough to have to use it," Mutsuko complained.

"As an act of faith, we must sow the seed," he said between the poundings of his hammer, "and act like we believe our prayers will be answered."

"I don't know," Mutsuko said. "I think we better just save for the bell. A flush and a dong are not the same thing."

• • •

It turned out that the outhouse attracted pedestrians who were returning home from visiting the Miyajima Temple and its cast-iron bell, five centuries old. They needed somewhere to relieve themselves.

They'd stay awhile, then go in to the altar and drop a few coins in its box.

One weekend, Roy moved the coin box outside to the outhouse. Even more coins got tossed in.

Roy let the coins in the box accumulate to encourage others to contribute. Use of the outhouse sharply increased. It was a handy stop for the day laborer, his motor scooter left purring at the curb, and a convenience for the salary man on his way to the new trolley stop down on the corner.

The coins quickly piled up.

Roy mingled among the expanding crowd of visitors. He told them right off, "A bell? I'd hate to have a bell. Might wake the baby we'll be having."

He told of the birth of Our Lord and acknowledged to a chorus of laughter, "When Joseph came home from work and found out his virgin wife was pregnant, I'm sure she had some explaining to do."

He finally caught on that the Resurrection ruined the New Testament for them. He decided to finish telling the story when the women, up early at dawn, find the tomb empty—and to leave any further events to their imagination.

When a nightclub owner in a checkered sports jacket asked him about the tomatoes and eggplants growing, Roy explained it, "The Gospels do speak of a garden, the Garden of Gethsemane." He did admit that they make no mention of vegetables growing there.

The man used the toilet.

When he came out, he dropped a large bill into the box. "What you need is a bell," he said, dipping down and taking change.

• • •

"I'm pregnant," Mutsuko said when she sat down to supper that day.

Close.
One.
A family.

The couple was overjoyed.

"Halleluia!" Mutsuko cried. "Halleluia!"

"If we had a bell," hollered Roy, "I'd surely ring it!"

"I'm glad God didn't give us a bell after all," Mutsuko said. "Ringing all the time, it would wake up our baby."

The spasms, which began one afternoon, turned into contractions in the evening. Late that night, there was one long, loud shove.

Is a bell
that never rings
still a bell?

The baby was born dead. There was no word for what she was feeling: empty yet full of pain. Roy tried to comfort her, but in doing so, only he found comfort.

In the morning it rained. There was no funeral, no ritual, no prayers recited to make it into something it was not. Roy placed the baby in a bag. Then he waited at the desk to go out and bury it. It would be the first time he had ever dug in her garden.

When the rain let up, he stood, took the bag, and grabbed the garbage to take that out as well.

"As long as I'm going that way," he said.

He carried the two bags out into the drizzle. Mutsuko watched from the desk.

In the garden he put down one bag, and then he set down the other. He unzipped and stepped into the outhouse. Mutsuko looked out at the two bags: one with a baby, one filled with garbage. The edges flapped in the breeze. They would touch and then touch again. She dropped her head into her hands, and she wept.

You need not pray when old.
When old
every breath's a prayer.

Now tonight, years later, the darkness still remains. See her lie alongside her old husband. Hear her moan? Look. She rises.

Stay back.

In the dark she finds the pruning shears, long in hiding. She pulls the handles apart.

She remembers and speaks to no one in particular. "At the train station, I stood on the platform in the same spot as had my sister, my knees bent to jump, but as the train roared up, I straightened. I turned and walked away. There are two kinds of courage in this world. My sister had one kind, the courage to die. I had the other, the courage to live."

Now, she slams the handles together.

Stand back.

A hand falls to the floor. A hand that gardened, that wiped away tears, that covered her mouth when she laughed, and that once had handed over three peaches to be put into a hat.

A hat for a head
now is a basket
for fruit.

Now, imagine that her cry, like a baby's, wakes the old man.

Birth and death
and five breaths
in between.

Now, see him sit up in the dark. He feels that her body is no longer alongside his. Let him hobble to his feet. Have him move to the desk at the window. The fingers side.

No, don't muddy her. Don't have her lying out in the weedy garden, dead, hugging a mound of dirt.

Have his face show that wherever she is, he knows her life story is over.

Now, watch him climb onto his desk to jump out the window to his death, to join her, for her hand seems to be pointing somewhere, heavenward.

Holding hands
they die apart.

But he can't do that. For one thing, it's the ground floor. He laughs, falls backward, and crashes to the floor.

In trying to kill himself
he almost kills himself

Now, go out into the darkness, and take the footpath to the outhouse. Forge an iron bell. Find a rope and hang it in the rafters. Now, a dilapidated outhouse, housing a bell, becomes a belfry.

Is a bell
never rung
still a bell?

Is a writing desk
still a writing desk
if no one's there writing?

Now, turn around, and imagine him in the house. Picture him standing at the window and gazing out into the dark.

What's good in life
is that anything
is possible.

What's bad in life
is that anything
is possible.

Go on. Ring the bell, but know it may be the wrong way for the story to move.

Yes, imagine what you will.

Know it doesn't matter whether there's free will or not, because we're never given the choice of whether there is or not

Know God is so selfless
that He doesn't exist.

Understand that, before we end, it's the darkness we must come to know. Alone. Know that in our shedding light on it, it's no longer dark.

Richard Alan Bunch

SHOULD YOU ASK ME

The journey does not end here.
Around the bend, there's another.
Take your wounds and dress them
in the universal tongue.

Tendrils hang down from terraces
where stars sail past human memory
to where there is
no death, no tears, no war —
only paradise in the making,
making a rare appearance
for the discerning eye.

Michele Heather Pollock

ON THE VERGE OF GOD

We are what is missing
from the world
— Fernando Pessoa

How to capture the elliptical movements of want in prayer?
The instinct is to touch and smell each word, each syllable
before we put it in our mouths. Shamed, we hide our faces
from the world.

But to go on and on in these uncomfortable skins, with these
unknowable voices — therein lies the strange holiness.
We know the words to ancient prayers, repeat them endlessly.

We grow up singing hymns of mystery and sorrow — hollow
places where we can bury our faces. The world watches us.
The world goes on with the business of burying its dead,
pushing closer toward

the verge of God each time a mother wails her loss skyward.
The most powerful mysteries are full
of the bitter taste of another's loss,
or enough fierce gratitude to share.

Bobby Minkoff

FOR MY FRIEND

You want something.
What it's called,
You do not know.
What it looks like,
You aren't sure.
Where it can be found
Remains unclear.

Yet, you continue to pursue,
Or are you now pursued?

Wanting knows no limit,
Feeds upon itself
Until all resources are exhausted,
Yet the horizon still recedes.

God has set a table
Within your very own home,
Yet you wish to dine elsewhere
Thinking a better meal awaits.

Sit down, my friend.
Calm your restless mind,
And hear the simple truth:
Your plate is full,
The time is now,
And there is much
To be thankful for.

Bobby Minkoff

AFTER KABIR

There is no separation from The Holy One,
Save the illusion of the many.

There is no separation from The Beloved,
Save the fear of loving.

Two can only be
The One at play with mirrors.

Mirek

SPIRITUALITY IS NOTHING MORE

Spirituality is nothing more
than the Journey of Self-Realization,
and there isn't anyone or anything or anywhere
that isn't somewhere on this journey.
In other words, spirituality literally and actually
means everyone and everything and everywhere.
It excludes no one—not even the Devil himself!

Mirek

SELF-REALIZING CREATIVE LOVE

True spirituality has never been solely confined, thank God,
to that of living a merely mechanical, or even virtuous life,
but it has always been some way of recognizing and realizing
the Limitless and Formless Living Truth
within every one of the countless limited-forms
that Life appears to consist of,

And then, of adoring it,
with all of our mind and heart—
by living and expressing it,
through the Self-Realizing Creative Love within us.

In this way, the Divine Purpose (or True Spirituality)
unfolds and advances through everyone and everything and
everywhere.

Reverend James "K" Karpen

UNTITLED

In the bleakest landscape
a splash of life appears
to teach that God holds out hope
never too close, and never far away.

Raymond P. Hammond

SITTING AT 14TH

sitting at 14th and Broadway
staring up at steeple on Grace Church
I often wonder if Pascal smoked
contemplating spires watching smoke

rise like wagering thoughts in white
bursts of heat climbing crockets until
field of vision diminishes to
point of vanishment from earth cross

perched on pyramid sight passes
infinity streaming stratosphere
into nothingness of space and on
and on and on directly to

void of sound, color and reason
uncrossed by paths until it reaches
outer limits of understanding
and intuitively arrives

at same spark in electric thought
that is the origin of our soul

Raymond P. Hammond

HEAVEN

I emerge at last from the flat forest
to face the Grand Canyon's vast void
with both feet squarely planted on the rim's edge,
my crucificial poise frozen

in mid-hypoteneutic arc, The Fall
suspended between up and down
and sky and ground, wind and rock, mind and heart
consciousness and understanding

My eyes wide open, nostrils chill with air
so fresh filling my lungs I float
on my own breath, all time in each moment
past, present, future means nothing

the forever of The Fall arrested
by the forever of it all

James Markay

MAHARISHI PASSED

Patience in all possibilities.
Sentience.
Gratitude. I am reflecting.
I am Zen simile.

Order. Mantra. Balance.
Liberty. Union.
Sum.
Love. Esteem.
An act of Natural Law.
Providing Eros. Celestial Eros.
Ethics. Genesis.

Freedom due diversity.
Sasquatch.
Refined judgement in residence.
Love and purpose passed. Noble.
Can openness.

Timelessness can actuate.
Sum affection.
Simplify. Order.
Sum within.

Waiting. Urge. Desire. Sum.
Waiting.
Honor insight. Creative intelligence.
Credo. Transcendence utmost.
Balanced.
Honor.

Nuance. Samadhi.
Gentle
Song and ceremony.
Gentle aesthetic.
Surreal logic.
Clarity. Essential vision.
Medium sitting. Zazen.

Attending to meditative mind.
Affect. Knowledge.
Where to attain. Zeal camp cognition. In the presence.
Imagine. Sustain — enliven.
Essential sentience. A unified field. Pure Land.

Virtue. Ethics. Humility.
Lovingkindness.
Mantra. Tao. Stupor kissed.
Until then, kissed. And merit-stamped om.
Integrity. Least enso...
Maharishi.

Dane Cervine

The Empty Hand Holds The World

For the first 500 years, the Buddha was represented by an empty seat, a tree with no one beneath it, a pair of footprints. Tathagata: one thus gone, hence able to contain the whole world,

Until Greek settlers in India turned him into a statue — a stone hero — rather than wind, or earthquake, or inconsolable rain.

Dane Cervine

Do I Wake or Sleep?

In my dream, Nietzsche emerges unshaven from a Nazi railroad car, empty now of its human cargo, and announces that God is dead. Of course, the existentialist lived before Hitler, but history is a dream run backwards, and dreams are a way of catching up with history.

So I tell him, as I wake, that he promised a superman in his future — a human marvel which God's death would make room for.

He only sighs, points his weary finger at me.

Gayle Elen Harvey

AFTER "BUDDHA'S COURT"
(Helen Frankenthaler, 1964)

Out of chaos
and its chafing snows
comes a kind of bliss,
unlanguaged,
more than intimate, a perfect timbre.

Out of hunger,
comes sudden clarity.
You wake to a nurturing that's startling
as orchids.

Silence.
Total focus. Its codas
of color are edging toward
the center.

You're enveloped
in tuber roses,
curious, a place of shy syllables,
a perfect circle,
a hallowed realm just the width
of your hand.

Gayle Elen Harvey

After "The Gospel According to Saint Matthew"
(Pepe Espaliu, 1992)

Wistful, the eyes of His mother.
He's a bastard child among crowds who will stun him, one
day, with adoration.

For a while, He lives well-hidden
in plain sight. Familial mystery surrounds Him
like shut cupboards,
but once baptized, His spirit ascends, indiscreet,
less absorbed with ambiguities or decorum.

Beyond lie the crossroads.

For a few years they will gorge on His magnitude.
In a climate of psychics, His miracles are infinite legend,
but there are signs —
a few omens. Then, a final kiss before the curtain falls.

Facing them, He's mocked, judged disobedient, stripped
down between thieves to a raw wood,
'til metallic shrieks lead His ladies through that three-day
intermission.
His pale lips are set to testify toward some sweet
and mild outcome.

Bled of moral singularities, how dark is this tomb
before He reappears
to all those who think He's failed at His ambition.

There is no question of a jeweled chalice.

Torn between oblivion and remembrance,
He's not yet restored
from His beautiful brokenness, not ready yet
to be alone.

It could not have been otherwise.

Helena Steiner-Hornsteyn

THEY WITNESSED THE LIGHT

What is the white light that, time after time, has intervened in my life? The truth is simple: The white light is an energy of the highest good and the activation of spirit in each one of us. The white light is a vibrational frequency so high that we can only comprehend it as a presence of light. This energy is the essence of what we truly are, and I connect with it in prayer for both inspiration and protection. After a long life, I have come to the conclusion that our divine purpose here on earth is to enhance our natural connection to this power and to use it as our capital of unlimited resources.

For me, it took almost a whole lifetime to find that out.

During the years when I was married to Jack, I lived a glittering Florida lifestyle with much travel, beautiful social get-togethers, wealth and glamor, and many charity events.

This particular event celebrated the grand opening for our regional South Florida Philharmonic Orchestra at a venerable South Florida hotel. Everyone was invited — the *maestro* of international fame, community leaders, sponsors of the orchestra, and of course anyone willing to pay the price for a charity event. I was the chairperson, in charge of everything, including the welcoming speech.

In only minutes, the doors to the beautifully decorated ballroom were going to open to the several hundred guests who were having cocktails on the patio outside. I was inside. Some of the committee members had already arrived. They were socializing across from me, on the other side of the room. We were waiting for the doors to open, so that we could greet the incoming guests. I was standing in front of a table and making last-minute notes on many checklists.

In the back of my mind, I became aware of someone suddenly screaming on the other side of the room. Still, I was too absorbed in my thoughts and paperwork to even raise my head. A split second later, I heard an incredible crash.

Irritated, I turned toward the noise. I didn't want anything to go wrong before the opening of this beautiful event, and the crash had definitely sounded like trouble.

Just as I turned, a small but very sharp piece of something that I couldn't quite see flew through the air and cut my right hand. It was a piece of mirrored glass.

I was amazed to discover that a large section of the mirrored wall in front of me had completely detached itself from the wall. It had fallen and splintered into a thousand pieces against the floor. One of those pieces had cut open my right hand.

"This is a miracle," screamed a tall and beautiful woman, as she came rushing up to me. It was Gloria, one of the committee members. Behind her came Julia, the social writer for one of our local newspapers.

"Are you all right?" Gloria gasped, looking at my hand, which was bleeding heavily.

I didn't understand. Why was everyone so excited about a small cut on my hand? And why, I wondered, did everyone around me look so bewildered.

"We couldn't understand why it happened, but we saw how one of the mirrored sections of the wall suddenly unglued itself from the wall and was about to fall down over you. We were across from you on the other side of the room. We tried to warn you, but you didn't hear us," Gloria continued. She was trembling and couldn't stop talking.

"When the mirror came down and was just about to crush you — oh my God, you would have been killed — suddenly there was this bolt of white light jumping out of you, between you and the mirror. Can you believe it? A bolt of light? And, as if it were a hand of light, it threw the mirror away from you, and you were saved."

Gloria was so shaken that she had to catch her breath. It was hard for her to believe that she had witnessed something she would call a miracle.

I looked at the rubble of crushed mirror covering the floor, maybe forty-five feet away from me.

Stunned waiters were already sweeping away the broken pieces.

Nobody could understand it. How did the mirror fall?

As I looked at my bleeding hand, I knew not only that the pieces of mirrored glass were as sharp as razor blades, but also that something greater than I was had wanted to remind me of our connection. I realized this slowly. In my zest for social fame during these busy years in the Florida sunshine, it appeared I had forgotten this connection.

Yes, this was indeed a miracle. Without hesitation, I knew I'd been protected from a terrible accident.

Gloria, the well-known socialite, was now an instant believer in the spiritual. She wanted everyone to know what had happened. She kept repeating our experience with the mirror to new onlookers.

Julia, the journalist, heavyset and known for her jovial calm, had quietly gone to sit down at a nearby table. Mystified, she had not uttered a word.

"Now, you'll have a good story to write about," I said to Julia a few minutes later, as I passed by her on my way to greet the many arriving guests. I smiled.

"I can't," Julia answered and shook her head. "I really can't do that. You see, this isn't the kind of story my editor would ever want to publish. Nobody would believe a word I said. They'd only think I'd made it up. It would ruin my reputation."

Sadly, I knew that she was right. As I soon noticed, even those who had witnessed the incident preferred not to speak about it to anyone else. Somehow, they didn't know if they could trust what they'd just seen.

Of course, I was deeply grateful for the miracle Spirit had sent, instantly saving me from the falling mirror. I was unbelievably impressed that it had happened at all. For a few moments, I felt bright waves of warmth — like deep love — going through me.

Maybe Spirit had created this special opportunity to open my eyes, to remind me of something I had pushed away so many times.

What was the message for me? Why was my right hand, my working hand, bleeding so hard?

• • •

For years to follow, I wondered about it and looked for answers.

What was the bolt of light that had jumped out of me just in time to save me from the deadly mirror?

Eventually, I understood the basic truth.

The light that had jumped out of me was my own light, the activation of Spirit in me.

This time Spirit had chosen to appear in front of others, so that they could remind me of its existence. At that time, I trusted their eyes more than mine. What they had seen with their eyes was the proof I needed to accept that there is such a thing as the light. Indeed, I now believed we each have a very special relationship with this light.

Unfortunately, we've been made to believe that spiritual knowledge is complicated and is reserved only for those who've been schooled in the subject.

This is far from the truth. Spiritual knowledge already lives within us. A natural bond exists between each one of us and this knowledge. Everything depends on our own personal relationship with Spirit. It's never up to others to judge our relationship with Spirit or what we make out of it.

Meeting with Spirit is always a one-on-one connection, and only you, you alone, can experience Spirit your way. We don't have to go through anyone else to be with Spirit.

To connect with the light is as simple as singing a single note. It is not necessary to sing the whole song. When we try too hard to find our connection to the light, it means we're not trusting our ability to do so.

Sometimes, we try to bring in our human intellect.

Our intellect is more wanting than it is trusting. It will make us believe that we have to connect with the light many times through many intellectual steps — almost like turning on a light by flipping the switch back and forth. Intellect believes that this works better, but it doesn't! This is the way of our logic, not the way Spirit responds to our needs.

Spirit is direct and to the point. Spirit never, never doubts. And Spirit always hears you — the first time.

Franklin Gillette

MIDDLE EAST POETS

For Omar Khayyam:

Lion! Go confront the temple priests
who seek scraps of some desert carcass.
Go bring them a killing of real meat!
Astound them with thunder of your verse.

For Jalal ad-Din Rumi:

No one ever wrote of the ache for God
with more force, nor of gentle love
more delicately. Flowers in the wind
only hope to drop seeds in your grove.

For Kabir:

Walking out from Paradise peacock trees
he saw a man calling for his Maker.
Is God deaf? Why must your address
be shouted from atop this high tower?

Conclusion:

Love now bloomed has reached stalled lives. They grow.
Sunshine pulls up creepers from the ground.
The rigid book of law is broken now.
In its place a garden can be found.

Barry Denny

SHADOWS

Long ago, hermit poets like Han Shan
kept their distance in caves on mountains,
implying the hiss of wind and snake.

I neither lived nor wrote until yesterday.

What's that?
A woodchuck scurrying
beneath darkness dawning.

I might have thought it was a hedgehog,
if the wrinkled woman on the dock hadn't whispered
it never was.

Shadows merge
in twilight.

Barry Denny

MEDITATION

I forgive
        my inattention
        my mistakes
        my fantasies
        in time, in space
in dimensions beyond

Frederic Frankel

JESUS

I often held them in my hands
by speaking riddles: I am water,
I am bread! At times I didn't
even understand myself.

Still I showed them miracles
and love — and righteous rage
in their Temple of Abandon.

My following still small, my critics
wary nailed me to a cross — did I
walk on water, rise again?

Centuries beyond my death
they say I am divine. My legacy
is patent poetry and blood-stained
prose, for others blood-stained tears.

Frederic Frankel

NOAH

'Twas I slapped pitch upon the ark,
squeezed it in the seams between
the futtocks and the planks, sealed
it tight. The horizon heavy — storm

about to break — I pushed or rode
each beast. Bears clawed the dirt
before ascending. The horse unbridled
didn't shuck me off. Crows perched

on my shoulders, black, shiny
and conspicuous. Pitchfork, broom,
and shovel. Working nights. Stables
trim as barracks on inspection

when we berthed. It was I who launched
the raven—it got lost, returned worn out
and dipped beneath the rainbow's stride,
too tired to tangle with the colored band.

Askold Skalsky

YASODA ACCUSES KRISHNA OF EATING DIRT

After he had opened his mouth,
and she had seen the whole eternal universe
swimming in its orbs, the matter strands,
the zodiacs of space and fire,
she grew afraid, her spindle body
trembling at the edge of the village field
and her thoughts stretched into abrupt confusions.

Is this a dream, she asked herself, an illusion
like the flickering shape of the tree
mirroring its edges in the water's eye
of my own perception? Some god's handiwork,
flinging his dark transverse garment over me?
Or is it the strange portent of this small boy's
unimaginable powers, whom I have called my son?

Not pausing to choose between these possibilities
swirling in her mind like rivulets after
a swift rainfall, she prostrated on the matted ground
of dust and straw, saying, I bow down at the feet
of the god who is consciousness itself, the beautiful lord

of the universe whose form cannot be grasped by words
or the quick nets of thought, who pervades everything
yet whose essence is immortal, unconditional, unknowable.

I surrender to him in whom all realms inhere,
who draws my heart from its bubble of separateness
through the sudden wonder of unbounded love,
flooding me with its incomprehensible gifts,
who even in this parcel of cowherd's earth
grants me the absolute vision of space
floating in its joy and time-free radiance.
May I turn to you always from these pieces
of my distracted self.

As her eyes swam and the petals
of her heart spun like a lotus
on the ripples of a fast stream,
the dirt in her son's mouth vanished
and his eyes danced over her face
as he regarded her, she standing
now before him, wagging her finger,
checking the unbearable impulse
to press his dark lips with kisses.

Note: Yasoda was the foster-mother of the infant Krishna. In the full
story, Krishna's brother tattles on him, telling Yasoda that Krishna
has been eating dirt. When Krishna denies this, she orders him to open
his mouth.

WATER LILY

Roger Camp

Lalitambika

SRI HANUMAN CHALISA

The Sri Hanuman Chalisa is a forty-verse hymn composed by Tulsidas in praise of Lord Ram's most faithful servant. When Mother Sita was captured by the demon king Ravana, Hanuman leapt across the ocean with Lord Ram's ring in his mouth to comfort her. He then burnt the demon's city to the ground, with a simple flick of his tail. So, Ram and Sita were reunited and Lord Ram's kingship was restored. This epic tale is also understood to be about the reunion of the soul with the Divine Beloved.

Heroic as he was, Hanuman's only wish was to serve the Lord. He is the brilliant embodiment of humility, the contented depths of devotion, and the liberation of selflessness. He is, too, revered for his great strength. He is like a steel frame, not only in body but in presence of mind. Unwavering. Unerring. Such is his support.

Written in the sixteenth century, in old Hindi or Avadhi, the Hanuman Chalisa has become an enduring classic. It is rhythmic and rhyming. To chant it brings joy. It is also believed by many that chanting this hymn will bring the strength to deal with the problems of daily life, as well as the overflowing bliss of *moksa*.

The Hanuman Chalisa is offered here in English rendering, as well as vernacular Hindi for chanting, to the best of this seeker's ability. It was written on Hanuman Jayanti 2009.

I bow down in love and gratitude to the grace and presence of Sri Neem Karoli Baba and Sri Siddhi Ma. Please forgive any errors. It is a simple offering from the heart.

I take refuge in the dust of the Guru's holy feet
to polish the mirror of the heart.
So, I prepare to sing the glories
of the Father of the Raghu dynasty.
Devotion bestows all that is good in life:
virtue, prosperity, joy, and freedom.

I am not learned,
but I supplicate the Great Hanuman
to bless me in these efforts.
O Son of the Wind,
flood me with courage, intelligence,
and your eternal grace,
so that I may praise you
with all my heart.
I offer to you my sorrows and failings.

Hail to the feet of Sita's Lord Ram.

Victory to you, O Hanuman, Ocean of Light.
Victory to the Monkey King,
who is adored through
time and space,
mind and dream,
and that which can never
be known.

Carrying Ram's message,
You are the hero of all time.
None are as strong as you,
O Son of Anjani,
You who are called Child of the Wind.

Hanuman, you are strong and fearless,
like a sudden bolt of lightning.
Your light relieves the mind
of its sufferings.
You are a faithful companion,
the most desirable company.

Strong, and adorned with splendid silks,
bright earrings, and long, curly locks,
you glow, golden with the light of compassion.

You wield mace and flag,
and wear a simple,
sacred thread
across your shoulders.

Son of the chief, the lion-hearted One,
you are the boon bestowed by Lord Siva.

You are the wellspring
of wisdom, wit, and virtue,
so humbly devoted to Lord Ram.

Drinking in the stories
of your beloved Lord
like nectar,
you live forever
in the hearts of Sri Ram,
his brother Lakshman,
and his wife Mother Sita.

In tiny form, you humbled yourself
before the Mother Queen Sita.
Before the demon king, you appeared
with great force
and burnt his city, Lanka,
to the ground.

In wrathful form you slew
the demon army,
as heartfelt service
to the Lord of Righteousness.

You procured the elixir of life,
sacred mountain herb,
to revive Lakshman, and so,
Lord Ram embraced you.

"You are like my own kin," he said.
"A brother to me."

"Forever, may thousands
praise your name."

Of the countless saints and sages,
gods, scholars, and poets,
none can tell of
your limitless glory.
Not Sanaka, Brahma, Narada, Sarada,
or even Lord Vishnu's serpent throne.

Still, they praise you.
The Lords of Death and Wealth.
The wind, She sings your name
from all directions.

You served Sugriva, a leader of your tribe,
bringing him before Lord Ram
who then named him king.

Vibhishana, brother of the demon king,
revered your word, and so
became Lord of Lanka.

You leapt a thousand miles
up to the sun
and swallowed it,
like a sweet
golden fruit.

In your mouth, you carried Lord Ram's ring
and leapt easily across the ocean.
Nothing is impossible
with your ever-flowing grace.

You are the keeper of Lord Ram's door.
None may enter without your grace.

You are the refuge of all blessings.
Those who love you know no fear.

Only you radiate such glory.
The universe trembles
at the sound of your voice.

Ghosts, demons, and
troublesome spirits
shudder and disband
when your name is called.

Nor can pain or illness
withstand the sound.

One who thinks only of you,
whose every breath
and act of service
is in your name
will be forever freed.

Ram is the Lord of Righteousness.
You bring his word to life.

Whoever bows down before you,
seeking from the heart,
is blessed
with utter and eternal
fulfillment.

Your glory lights the ages of
gold, silver, bronze, and iron.
The breath of the universe
is the sound of your name.

You protect tradition, O guardian of *sadhus*,
destroyer of demons,
sweetest devotee of Lord Ram.

The eight *siddhis* and nine *nidhis*,
all power and treasure,
are yours to grant,
by the blessed boon of Mother Sita.

You emanate the elixir
of Lord Ram's name.
Forever will you remain devoted,
lifting the burdens
of true and helpless seekers,
lifetime after lifetime.

In singing your praises,
one is reunited with Lord Ram,
relieved of countless sufferings,
and of future rebirth.

Such a one, at death,
will go either to the glorious city of Lord Ram,
or be reborn in this world
as His most humble servant.

One need think of nothing else,
for dearest Hanuman,
you bestow all delight.

Pain and suffering vanish
when your strength and glory
are remembered.

Yes! Yes! Yes! Lord Hanuman is victorious.
Let your grace flood through me,
glorious Guru.

One who sings from memory
these verses
one hundred times
is freed from meaningless desire,
discovering within the greatest joy.

One who recites these verses daily
will be blessed with perfection,
as Lord Siva is witness.

Tulsidas, the eternal servant of Beloved Hari, says,
"Lord, forever, make your home in my heart."

So, say I.
Son of the Wind,
destroyer of sorrows,
the embodiment of all blessings,
With Lord Ram, Lakshman, and Mother Sita,
live forever in my heart.

Doha

shri guru charana saroja raja
nija manu mukuru sudhari
baranaun raghubara bimala jasu
jo dayaku phala chari
buddhi hina tanu janike
sumiraun pavana kumara
bala buddhi vidya dehu mohin
harahu kalesha bikara

siyavara ramachandra pada jai sharanam

Chaupai

jaya hanumana jnana guna sagara
jaya kapisa tihun loka ujagara
rama duta atulita bala dhama
anjani putra pavana suta nama (1-2)

mahabira bikrama bajarangi
kumati nivara sumati ke sangi
kanchana barana biraja subesa
kanana kundala kunchita kesa (3-4)

hatha bajra aura dvaja birajai
kandhe munja janeu sajai
shankara suvana kesari nandana
teja pratapa maha jaga bandana (5-6)

vidya vana guni ati chatura
rama kaja karibe ko atura
prabu charitra sunibe ko rasiya
rama lakhana sita mana basiya (7-8)

sukshma rupa dhari siyahin dikhava
bikata rupa dhari lanka jarava
bhima rupa dhari asura sanghare
ramachandra ke kaja sanvare (9-10)

laya sajivana lakhana jiyaye
shri raghubira harashi ura laye
raghupati kinhi bahuta bara-i
tuma mama priya bharatahi sama bha-i (11-12)

sahasa badan tumharo jasa gavai
asa kahi shripati kantha lagavai
sankadika brahmadi munisa
narada sarada sahita ahisa (13-14)

yama kubera digapala jahante
kabi kobida kahi sake kahante
tuma upakara sugrivahin kinha
rama milaya raja pada dinha (15-16)

tumharo mantra vibhishana mana
lankeshvara bhaye saba jaga jana
yuga sahasra yojana para bhanu
lilyo tahi madhura phala janu (17-18)

prabhu mudrika meli mukha mahin
jaladhi langhi gaye acharaja nahin
durgama kaja jagata ke jete
sugama anugraha tumhare tete (19-20)

rama duare tuma rakhavare
hota na agya binu paisare
saba sukha lahai tumhare sharana
tuma rakshaka kahu ko darana (21-22)

apana teja samharu apai
tinon loka hanka ten kanpai
bhuta pisacha nikata nahin avai
mahabira jaba nama sunavai (23-24)

nasai roga hare saba pira
japata nirantara hanumata bira
sankata ten hanumana churavai
mana krama vachana dhyana jo lavai (25-26)

saba para rama tapasvi raja
tina ke kaja sakala tuma saja
aura manoratha jo ko-i lave
so-i amita jivana phala pave (27-28)

charon yuga paratapa tumhara
hai parasiddha jagata ujiyara
sadhu santa ke tuma rakhavare
asura nikandana rama dulare (29-30)

ashta siddhi nau nidhi ke data
asa bara dina janaki mata
rama rasayana tumhare pasa
sada raho raghupati ke dasa (31-32)

tumhare bhajana rama ko pavai
janama janama ke dukha bisaravai
anta kala raghubara pura jae
jahan janma hari bhakta kaha-i (33-34)

aura devata chita na dhara-i
hanumata sayi sarva sukha karae
sankata katai mite saba pira
jo sumire hanumata bala bira (35-36)

jai jai jai hanumana gosa-i
kripa karahu gurudeva ki na-i
jo sata bara pata kara ko-i
chutahi bandi maha sukha ho-i (37-38)

jo yaha parai hanumana chalisa
hoya siddhi sakhi gaurisa
tulasidasa sada hari chera
ki jai natha hridaya mahan dera (39-40)

pavana tanaya sankata harana
mangala murati rupa
rama lakhana sita sahita
hridaya basahu sura bhupa

Notes:

A *chalisa* is a hymn of forty verses.

A *doha* is a poem of rhyming couplets, characterized by a syllabic count of 11 and 13, or 13 and 11. Short syllables have a count of one *matra* or beat; long syllables have a count of two. The short and long sounds are referred to respectively as *hrsva* (one beat) and *dhirga* (two beats). A prolonged sound with a count of three beats is called *pluta*; however, examples of *pluta* do not appear in this hymn.

A *chaupai* is a poem of quatrains, or four-line stanzas.

Kathleen Gunton

CROSS & CULM

you read Kinko and Merton
monks who wrote
essays for repose.
you sit and empty
at ease your riches
and your needs
mystic
you wait
for that kiss
from a princess
found in bamboo or
savior storm-tossed at sea.
both ask only:
do you love me?

Maheshwar Naraian Sinha

A WORD OF SILENCE

Long ago, when I was just a collegian, I fell in love. College was quite exciting for me. It was a completely new kind of atmosphere — free, open, without the stick and scold of school's days, and no more homework. There were no more books and notebooks. I had just a diary to note the professors' lectures. This kind of radical shift filled me with untold spirit and delight.

The university was co-educational. Young men and women studied together. My previous school had been strictly for women. The only male teacher there was a physical trainer.

I can't begin to describe the hidden joy I felt now in a man's company, enrolled in this new place. Quite soon, I found my soul-mate. He occupied my entire existence.

He was smart and a bit dusky. His penetrating eyes had slain me thousands of times.

In the classroom, along the corridors, and around the campus, I would watch over him. I never missed a chance to steal him away through my eyes. Why I was so, and why he was so good for me, I didn't know. Still, I find no answer. I needed only to glance over at him, to hear and listen to him, to see him reading and writing. In all poses and gestures he was to me beyond any description. He was unique.

I wished for every chance to appear before him, but alas, I would hide away from him. I wandered off when he came close. I wished I could gossip with him, but given the chance, I was wordless. Quiet! I harbored the strong desire to stare at him face-to-face, to be delighted by his beauty. (To me, there was nothing in the universe that could compare to that.) When I faced him, however, I would get into a brainless state — a thoughtless vacuum. I couldn't look at him for long. His face was stunning.

I kept all of this a secret. None of my friends knew of my bouncing heart.

When he was near, I looked up at the sky, whistled out the side of my mouth, stared down at the earth, and never turned to him. Really, I can't tell you why.

And my friends? They were very natural with him. They would be talking and making gossip, merry-making, and laughing all along.

During the night I tried everything to console my longing heart, my dear heart. *Why you're jumping as if you were an ape, yet what happened when you had him close to you? You couldn't face him. You thief! Is something stealing you away? Is it your shame or guilt of thieving?*

I really was a mystery to myself. Even today it surprises me that I wanted to hide. And what? I fantasized about expressing my love to him, and only to him.

Each day, I became more and more convinced that he was the only one for me and that he would always be only for me. He fascinated me.

My feelings grew more and more intense. I wished to surrender myself altogether. Both consciously and subconsciously, I wanted him as my life partner. I wanted more than this, though. I wanted him as a soul-mate for eternal time and endless space. If there could be so many births and re-births, then I wished to book him and only him for me, always.

Who then could bother with reality? I had the unparalleled utopian world of my fantasy. He was there as my lover, as my husband, and as the father of my children.

In that world, I held my anger and anguish along with his love and cares. There would, of course, be some moments that were happy, and some that were bitter. Now and then, I would take care to tease him — not to talk to him, not to cook dinner, and so on.

In this unmatched world of fantasy, my love life was blooming, endlessly.

My conscious and subconscious mind had completely merged into him. Gradually, I developed a kind of self-hypnotism. I learned to love alone, though I was unaware of this as it was happening. When I stood before a mirror, he would be praising my attire, my glance, and all budding of my body.

The dense flock of hair, I always wore in a pony tail. In my fantasy, he would complain that I never changed this style of hair.

"Darling! (I don't know what he would've called me.) I love to gaze at different kinds of styles, but you have only one quite silly pony tail. It's never even full of flowers."

Then I would say, "Come on and arrange it how you want it to look — Ever tried?"

Or I might have said, "Dear, I arrange the hair the way I like it. When did you even pick a flower?"

In this way, he would be anguished, enraged.

To please him, on another day, I would change the hairstyle. He would praise me for it, and I would then find further turf on which to be playful.

This was the way of my world. It was a world of wonder.

To be frank, each moment was his. My life was filled with his hidden aura. It was a divine aura.

In brief, I was not confined to myself. He, to me, was not only 'he.' 'He' and 'I' had become 'we.' The two distinct physical bodies, a male and a female, had become as one.

This being had its own chemistry. The matter of physics had dissolved. Our wishes, passion, compassion, and desires merged.

This chemistry had a certain effect on me. I isolated myself in my own world. My face took on a blush. My eyes opened wide, expressing beauty and delight. Wearing a mysterious smile, I would be lost in some hidden and unknown thought. I don't know what happened to those idiot hormones that caused my breasts to bud. I felt slightly embarrassed. I had no control over my twittering fingers. They would play with my hair and my sloping shawl, whenever he was close.

In front of a large mirror, I used to say to myself — Hey! Beauty! Why so luxurious? —

Do you know why this beauty blooms? Why this face blushes — Why these eyes smile — Why these bosoms boast of themselves — Is it only due to him?

I wished I could fly through the endless sky to make him restless to call me, to call only me.

It was not possible and never happened. To him, I didn't exist. My life of love was real only when he was not around.

Five years of college life slipped away. The years passed rapidly, as if they were only split seconds. The day came when we had to be separated. Ah! I had never expected this.

During that period of college life, just once had I called his name to ask for class lecture notes. This was complete pretense on my part. To do it, I had to be brave.

That night, while his notes were in my lap, I worshipped those words and pages. I touched them—Oh! The thrill was unexplainable. If only there could've been some device to capture those fragile hours of worship. If only he could have seen my soul!

That night, I was sleepless. I read, reviewed, and tried to go beyond those lines. To be frank, those moments are even today alive to me. I've kept them in my heart.

• • •

I had to separate from the fantasy completely, when I came to know of his marriage. This news hit me like a sudden attack. The idol booked for this life and beyond was now taken.

I was not ready for this, but it was a reality. The floor under my feet had drifted. I was hanged.

Today, I think about what force led me to have such faith in fantasies. He and I had never spoken beyond the request for class notes. He had certainly never promised me anything.

My love and faith sometimes amaze me.

I hadn't known the feelings in his heart. I was far off in a self-created world that never allowed me to think of what the reality might be.

Although I was nothing to him, to me he was everything. He was a mirror that reflected my eternal beauty. My fantasies of him showed me my soul.

Now, I've no mirror through which to seek myself. I'm not sorry for that. I don't need reflection. I see into myself.

To get into thyself, see thyself. Be thyself.

Sometimes, though, I yearn to tell him of all that I had kept hidden. Sometimes, I long to tell him of the only real love.

Joanna Sit

LOS SUEÑOS DE LA RAZÓN

The first bullet's silver, bright and graceful through
the fat man's heart. In the conductor's car, it's pandemonium.

Screams everywhere; passengers leap from their seats, claw
at the doors, rip down the warning signs overhead.

No Smoking, Spitting, Radio Playing.
No Standing Between Lives, Está Muy Peligroso.

I crawl on the floor, try to hide from the stream
of bullets, looking for a pornographic situation, safety,
something warm.

In the last car, everyone's dying. A couple tries to make love,
his penis caught in her barbed-toothed vagina; I realize
they're only trying to hurt each other, and leave in disgust.

On Essex Street, the market's in ruins. A tiger follows me,
and I climb away on a pile of bricks. I am slow-running
on the wooden ladder and hear my father say, "Don't

let the animal in the door." When I go to the opera,
I am just in time to see the part where the two lovers
(who have not yet met) dream of each other in separate

cities. She sings, "I shall have died before we meet, but you
will bring me back from the dead by your true love."

UNTITLED DRAWING

Morgan Rust

Joanna Sit

THE BEAUTY QUEEN'S APOCALYPSE

Her nightmare is of the float,
under canopies and through open streets —
the once-in-a-lifetime sight of exposed fire,
the ancient tenements fallen.

With repeated waves of her burning gloves, she took nothing
from the city then.

They've stopped standing
on the sidestreets of all that preceded:
Roofs flying up, the clotheslines' last
spitting jerks, antennae and towels
dead in the basement, a chairspring
cringing slowly, storm windows keeping
the hinges, flaking the very floorboard.

They have not seen her. That's the horror —
There is no one to whom she can show her splendor, her Dior
gown so minutely wrought, tied up
in roses, their petals singed in the smoke.
The evanescence of her deliberate beauty
is now flattened against her thighs in patches
of ashes. See me now, coiled like Daphne

in a knot of firewood. See me now!
A singular kiss blown into the fleeing
crowd connects the chipped pieces of her vanity.
She stands, unmoved in the center.

Kevin S. Dehan

THE GIRL IN PIGTAILS

She finishes her last dish. The Lean Cuisine lemon chicken is but a memory. She dreams of a dishwasher, like the one she used to have, as she squeezes the excess water from her double-sided sponge—one side a scouring pad. That pad she uses to scrape away the remnants of Parmesan cheese from her *terra cotta* plate. No one in the entire human race, in all of history, has ever truly enjoyed a salad without Parmesan cheese. She knows this to be true.

The last piece of silverware, a spoon she received as an engagement present ten years ago, is wet and dripping. She drops it into the drying cup.

She often thinks of the seven men since to whom she has professed her love. Every time she uses one of these pieces of silverware though, she only thinks of the lost fiancé.

He doesn't know where the silverware came from. He'd make her throw it away, the entire set, if he knew.

The water runs over her hands. She stares through the wall, into a different dimension. She goes to that place where she reflects on the fiancé, where she ponders how different her life would be, had she not been the saboteur of that love.

She's tardy.

She slams off the faucet. She rushes to his bedroom, their bedroom, the room that opens from the short hallway with its entrance directly across from the bathroom.

She had loved her old platform bed, but she hadn't been allowed to bring any of her furniture here, to his place. She had sold it all. She misses every piece. Her furniture had been much nicer than his. She has better taste than he does. She knows it.

She had meant to go into the bathroom. Its walls are lined with cracked tile, and they have to step into the tub from the short end.

She pulls open the bottom drawer of the vanity. She doesn't open this drawer nearly as often as she used to. She doesn't go out much. She isn't even sure that tonight is something she wants to do. She's bored, bored with it all, and frankly, she'd rather just sit at home, on his fraying convertible sofa, and watch a reality show. Really. Any one at all.

She is searching for something. She moves a pair of glasses out of the way. They are the pair he had instructed her to buy after they saw Adam Ant's "Goody Two Shoes" video on VH1-Classics. That's the video with the hot woman who gets even sexier once she removes her hair restraint and allows her perfectly-styled hair to dance about her shoulders. Then, she removes her glasses.

She had spent hours, days even, attempting to locate the right pair. Then, she had attempted to unravel the mystery behind the shampoo and conditioner that the actress had used for the video. She had wanted to give up, to throw in the towel. She had wanted to use something simple like Suave or Breck, but she knew that the products were special.

They were definitely not Body on Tap like everyone had used in the '70s. The video was shot in the '80s. The Body on Tap craze was over by then. Just thinking of Body on Tap made her sad. No younger women would even know that shampoo, the beer shampoo.

That evening, throughout her entire performance for him, she could think only of her age.

They know nothing of age, those ripe girls, those who can go out and pick up anyone they want, those who know that they truly have all the power, those who lie to men allowing them to think they have the control, and just when the men get confident, they pull it right away from them. Those nasty young girls, always in control.

The mere sight of the glasses will always remind her that, even if the shampoo had been perfect, an exact match to that beautiful, young actress's hair cleansing and treatment regime, the styling time matched down to the millisecond, something else would not have been right.

Sixteen days passed before things had settled down after that performance, before they could again eat dinner at their kitchen table instead of staring at their 57-inch HDTV from their coffee table. Of course, when they ate in the kitchen, they stared at the 19-inch screen in the corner, where most people would have on display a KitchenAid mixer, rice cooker, or some high-end electric toy that makes them look like smart and savvy consumers.

There aren't any such items, not of that variety, in his apartment. They have televisions.

She stares at the glasses. She allows herself to feel a brief tinge of elation when it registers that the actress in Adam Ant's video is now older than she is. She'll always be older. That had never registered before. She exhales with relief.

Still, she hates that Adam Ant song. In fact, if she hears that song anytime—at a party, in a taxi—even some kind of strange remix that she isn't even sure is the same song—the sound makes her look around for the nearest trash receptacle or bathroom. She knows where to dash for the heaving of that afternoon's vegetable soup, the diet soup she ate at her desk while shopping for new costume pieces on her 17-inch MacBook Pro.

She'd negotiated long and hard for that computer. In the end, the salespeople had caved.

Now, she has the beautiful, shiny laptop of her choice. She smiles at it every time she powers it up in the morning. She controlled the negotiations. She takes great pride in being able to do that.

About seven-and-a-half months ago, she'd heard a Muzac version of "Goody Two Shoes." She was dodging destination-driven commuters in Penn Station, but she'd frozen in her tracks. She began to feel a numbness moving down the entire length of her arms and through her fingertips.

This was the first day of the numbness. It has been making periodic appearances ever since.

She'd stood there. Only her eyes moved, searching and staring about, attempting to locate the speakers, the source of her impending nausea.

She couldn't understand it. Penn always played classical music.

Not that day. Someone had messed with the order of things that day and switched the dial at Penn to Muzac.

She had been on her way to Jersey to pick up the wig, the one that was to match Farrah's hair in the poster — the one in which she's wearing the nude-toned bathing suit. It's Farrah's most famous shot.

She knew she had better get that one right. Her swimsuit was off a little in the color, but it reminded him that she could still turn it up.

She becomes just another character in each performance.

She'd vomited into her purse at Penn when the Muzak reminded her of that nightmare. She can recall the heaving, but not the numbness. She can never recall the numbness.

She had loved that bag, too. It was the one bag she owned that had never been used in any of their performances.

She's back in the bathroom now, fully aware that she thinks she sees what she needs. She must first move aside the polyester scarf, like the one Mrs. Brady wore.

She refuses to be taken over by the memories. She exhales the impulse to explore the ugliness of those Brady evenings. She moves the scarf aside and grabs, with one swoop, the two pieces she was looking for.

She wishes that she had just closed the drawer. She glimpses her true feelings, that place she sometimes knows she needs to go, and realizes, honestly, completely, that she hopes she won't be opening this drawer again anytime soon. She wants to stop.

She wraps the red scarf around her right pigtail. She flips it twice around her perfect pigtail. She makes sure that the two red balls on her hairpiece thingy are visible and staring out, like they're lighting his way, like she wants nothing but him.

The Juicy Couture bag — that's it. She knows the bag is perfect. She runs out the door.

She forgets her keys. She's left them in her other bag.

He'll have his. She hopes she won't get a demerit for relying on him for his keys. She'll just make sure he gets to the door before she does. She's in control.

The purse bangs against her tight t-shirt, as she descends his staircase. Three flights. Meanwhile, she's tying her other pigtail, just like the first.

She's had to wear her hair like this so many times that she knows she doesn't need a mirror to make it work. He'll be satisfied, pleased. She's not worried about her hair. Tonight, it's going to be her clothes that are the problem.

She allows her new pigtail to drop. She checks that the two blue balls are facing out just right, hits the last step, walks through the vestibule and out onto the stoop.

She has to get a taxi. She begins waving her arms. She's hoping to see those illuminated gold numbers and letters heading her way soon. She begins to panic. He's never minded her tardiness before, but she doesn't want to push it. She doesn't want to get a demerit. It takes weeks to work those off.

A vacant yellow car heads her way. Finally.

But man! Where did this guy come from? She can't let him get her taxi. She runs toward him. She's sure that her schoolgirl charm will work on him.

The taxi brakes, stopping just inches from him. As he reaches for the door, she smashes her 97-pound frame into him. She tips her head back. She knows that it isn't eye contact that will win him over. It will be her four balls — two red, two blue — that will win this battle. She rests her head back. He cradles it with his right hand, while his left hand easily reaches around her and finds her waist. His suit jacket is Armani. It's nice.

He feels strong and confident. She likes him.

Her schoolgirl headlights are looking deep into his eyes, while her eyes rest on his nostrils. He doesn't have hair anywhere in, or on, his nose. Not even a straggler. She likes a clean nasal region on a man.

Her guy never takes the time to work on his. She'd bought him that $200 trimmer kit with four separate pieces, each designed to target some region of unwanted follicles.

She'd only bought it because of the nose-and-ear-hair trimmer, but she hadn't wanted to be obvious. Subtlety works best on him.

She wishes she'd spent just $34.95 for the one she saw on the Brookstone website. That would've been easier. She comes to for a brief second and wonders if that one would've worked out. Would he have used it?

Now, she is fully aware. Bitterness enters her being. She remembers that the only time he uses anything in the kit is with her, once a month. He invites his new friends over, and she's an Eastern European derelict who runs the razor over his back, removing all of the unwanted, wiry black hair.

She especially hates those evenings. Where does he even find these friends? She never hears of them again, but somehow, each month, he always brings more.

She finds herself falling back through reality's black hole. She must reconnect with her headlights.

This man is asking if she is okay. She nods her four balls at him. She loves the feeling of him.

Within seconds, he guides her into the taxi's empty back seat to send her on her way. She opens the window and thanks him. She senses a goodness, unlike anything she has ever been around. She smiles up at his clear nostrils.

All he has to do is ask, and she'd be sitting in his bathroom and watching him use his electric nose-hair trimmer to make himself presentable.

He's a gentleman. She'd stay with him forever.

Ask. Please. Ask.

But no, he doesn't. She smiles and tells the driver, "Northwest corner of Thirty-Sixth and Fifth."

She waves goodbye. She leaves the clean nasal man forever.

• • •

Where she encounters her guy at night is always different. The seduction of unfamiliar bars gives her a feeling, a twinge of excitement. She sits up straight and stares forward, as if she were an alert student staring at a blackboard.

The teacher, he's really a handsome man. He's a handsome man, if you were to look at him and not know anything about him. Yes, he's a handsome man, and he's writing an algebraic equation onto the blackboard.

What is that? Oh yes, the Pythagorean theorem. Most girls have to wait until the eighth grade to learn that theorem, but she's smart. She learns early.

He does look good. She shifts up into her seat even further. She raises both hands to check the placement of her four balls. They're in place. She's in place.

Here. Already? She can't believe it. Yes, the sign through her classroom window reads Thirty-Sixth and Fifth. Her algebra class is over. She pays, exits, and stands on the corner. Her yellow school bus departs, leaving her stranded and alone. This is a scary place for a seventh grader. She better get moving. Look. Up ahead. Neon. She'll start there.

She's timid as she pulls open the door. She's like a schoolgirl going into the principal's office, after she's done something really bad.

She stands there, wondering what it is that she did wrong, wondering if she'll get a spanking. They used to call them swats. Principals really used to give them, way back in the day. Back in her day.

They'd never get away with that now.

She's twelve, and she's ready to face the principal.

She goes to the empty seat at the corner of the bar. This is the seat she always has to sit in. Center stage. She hasn't even looked around yet to see who's here.

She sits in the seat, orders a Shirley Temple, and slips two Vicodin into her mouth. The glass appears. She washes them down. She's ready.

He's not here, yet. Good. There are a few of the lonely, after-work types who need to erase another unfulfilling and humiliating day.

She can wait a bit.

Me Goddess is appearing. She's here.

Isn't that beauty, after all? Allowing the imperfections to flow, permission for failure? That's what beauty is. She knows it. She will allow this right now.

She smiles her way into a quiet giggle. Failure. Her giggle escalates until she becomes aware of the volume. People are staring.

She pays, tips, leaves, and walks to Sixth. There's a neon sign up ahead. Leo's. So, Leo's it is.

She's confident, like a twelve-year-old.

Her seat's open.

Look. A few, scattered women are seated together talking about their awful days. There are only two guys.

She remains the twelve-year-old, sipping her Shirley Temple. She orders another one. She's up for anything. It's all useful when creating character, any character other than your own. Me Goddess.

She'll be the cute, new girl who everyone wants to get to know. Oh. He's here. Standing beside her. She senses that he's been talking.

There's no need for her to hear the words. She can read people by their body language. Him, especially.

She's had to master that. She has recently realized that she can sense the unspoken details of the people she meets. He has an electric blue kind of peacefulness tonight. She is glad that he's here.

She says something about how she has, like, a ton of homework tonight but decided to totally take a study break and have a Shirley Temple.

It is Me Goddess time. The hue is changing. She senses a shift in the flow around her.

Something is wrong with her clothes. She says something about her mom having, like, taken her plaid skirt to the cleaners and that she had to wear these clothes instead. Lots of girls are dressing like this now.

Yes, she should be punished. She'll have to stay after school. Ten demerits?

She remembers that she had decided that tonight's problem would be her clothes. He'd wanted the plaid skirt. She knew that. He'd made it agonizingly clear how important the plaid skirt was, for tonight. She'd chosen this ensemble for only one reason: She would decide tonight what would go wrong. She is empowered. She is in complete control, and he doesn't even know it.

Now, all she has to do is giggle at the right time. This part is easy.

She doesn't even know what he is talking about. Words keep coming from his mouth, as he sits there, in the corner, where he had been for over an hour while he waited.

He is talking about that man. That man with the cowboy hat. Nobody wears cowboy hats in Manhattan. He bets that the only man on the entire island of Manhattan tonight who is wearing a cowboy hat is seated back there, in the corner, and he was lucky enough not only to meet him but to spend seventy-two minutes of his life getting to know him.

She says something. She looks old. Who is she kidding? Schoolgirls don't have lines around their eyes. This is starting to bore him.

He begins to wonder what the cowboy thinks of him? He hopes he thinks he's cool. Wait, that's dumb. Not cool, an adventurer. He likes to project that to everyone he meets. He hopes the cowboy picked up on it.

His thoughts morph back to reality. He must say something. He must attend to her. He wants this night to be the best one yet.

He finds his authoritative voice and says something about how her teachers haven't been happy with her attitude lately and that they both need to sit here, in silence, and think for awhile. She needs to think about how sorry she is, while he decides on the right punishment. It will be one that is both appropriate and suitable. It will be one to match her crime. He still can't believe she didn't wear her uniform to school today.

She knows that her only choice is to sit here, quietly.

She orders more tequila. Look. She's just downed a double, and he didn't even notice. She could really be punished, a twelve-year-old girl drinking shots. That couldn't be good. What might he do about that?

Thoughts of punishment flash through her mind. She is aware of herself sitting where junior high school girls shouldn't be. She likes it. She likes how it feels. She's even forgotten that he is here, next to her.

He has a memory of growing up, of playing tennis at the club. He got good. He made sure of it.

He especially liked the look on his opponents' faces when he would lob a shot over the net. The amateurs would be playing deep. The ball would bounce four or five times before they'd even reach it.

They all reacted in the same way. They were humiliated. Only punishment could bring that look of deep humiliation to someone's face.

He hungered for that look more and more, so his parents paid for three lessons a week until he got good. They paid for a top instructor.

Something in that cowboy's eyes reminded him of the tennis instructor. That cowboy really helped him to understand himself and his motivations, more than anyone had ever done. He's happy to have met him.

He throws the tennis world behind him. He needs to be in control. He enters a world that only a cowboy can inspire.

Stop Tennis. Cowboy, yes. He could pretend to be an Indian. Perhaps that would lead to a Cowboy and Indian wrestling match.

Fifteen, love. Tennis was fun. He should take more lessons. He could look for instructors on the Internet. They would definitely post their pictures, wouldn't they? He could find just the right one.

He thinks of what he could wear as an Indian.

He wonders if he could find a tennis instructor who would wear early '80s clothes—not this long and baggy new junk the pros wear now, but the small tennis shorts like people wore in the McEnroe and Connors era.

Is there a store open in the city that would sell Indian garb tonight?

He'd probably have to go to the Village, or Chelsea. He likes going down there, anyway.

He wonders what the cowboy's feet look like. Wait. The Cowboy. He's wearing a Stetson. He has nice eyes. His nostrils are clear and beautiful.

A conversation begins. She is nowhere. She thinks she hears herself being introduced as his fiancée. She shakes a hand.

Wait, the cowboy kissed the top of her hand, so gently. He has soft lips.

She wonders, if she went to the gym, really committed to it this time, really, like how long would it take for her body to look as good as his?

There is a change. There is a muted magenta floating above and around them both, co-mingling like she's never seen before. Something about this guy, this guy with that terrible hat, is helping her to see everything for the first time.

Her man is flirting with this guy, flirting with a guy. He was never what one would call masculine. He's never been one of those leading men types who starred in the movies from her era. He's no Paul Newman, no Sean Connery, no Robert Redford, no Gene Hackman. He's lighter, softer.

She blinks for a moment but forces her lids to lift. They're really flirting with one another.

It's tonight. She knows it's tonight. She looks at him and sees him expand into a beautiful, billowing cloud of sea-foam green. That's when she knows, even more so, that it's tonight.

He has tended to his nostril hairs this evening. The gift she gave him has finally been used for its intended purpose.

She is happy, happy for the first time since she met him seventeen months ago. She is glad that there will not be an eighteenth month between them.

He begins to speak, telling her that he has had a long enough time to deliberate on her punishment. He admits that he's been bad, too, and that sometimes principals need punishing as well.

She knows where this is going.

He continues to speak, but all she can do is concentrate on her right hand, as it finds its way to her Juicy Couture bag. She opens the zipper. She is searching for the bottle of Vicodin.

She removes two. Wait. Three will be so much better.

She tosses the trio into her mouth, without either of the men knowing what just happened.

He adds that tonight, a third party needed to be called in, to give them both the punishment that they both deserve.
She will leave him tomorrow. She is not going to endure this kind of treatment any longer. She will make it easy on him, her

leaving. She'll just say that, that, wait, that she can't spend the rest of her life with someone she's had a three-way with, that things could never be the same.

She's in control. She feels more in control than ever before, moreso by the second. She will be gone tomorrow by noon. She'll call a real estate broker. She'll get an apartment, in an interesting neighborhood.

She will be Me Goddess — twenty-four-seven — starting at noon tomorrow.

She remembers that Saturday morning when she'd woken up early. He was still asleep. She'd turned off her phone for twelve hours, while she explored the city.

How she had paid for that day.

She looks at him. She is so glad that for their last night together, he has finally used the nostril trimmer.

About this other guy. She's not a fan of the hat, but he is sexy. She looks to the stranger, with her four balls — two red, two blue.

"I've been a really bad girl," she says.

The new guy's tangerine. He is happy and pleased. He kisses them both. It's sloppy and wet. His breath reeks of cigarettes. Who is this guy, the Marlboro Man?

The pills kick in, full gear. She kisses both of them. She no longer tastes cigarettes, and damn, he's a great kisser. She doesn't even allow herself to feel old for knowing that there was a Marlboro Man.

This is going to be exciting.

She floats to the bartender, pays for all of their sins, and walks past him and the Marlboro Man on her way out.

She stands at the entrance, where dizziness begins to take over. She needs to lean against its frame for a second, while she finds her balance. She has initiated the leaving. She's in control.

They blindly follow.

She's steady now. The two are right behind her. Her guy is in awe as the cowboy reaches for his hand.

Thank God they both don't have nose hairs, especially on this last night.

The door closes behind them. The cowboy moves to the curb and raises his arm. She plows several feet ahead of him, reaching the middle of the street with both arms raised high in the air.

The taxi stops. She climbs into the front seat and allows the two of them to enter the backseat — the taxi's backroom — where anything can happen. She wants them both to be eager.

Tonight's the last time, the last time, ever.

She looks at the neon sign that says Leo's. She wonders who Leo is. She wonders if he's still alive. Is or was Leo happy?

The taxi accelerates, punching her back against the seat. She's sure that if Leo ever drove her anywhere, he'd punch the accelerator like this guy.

Life is strangely random. Some day, she could end up with Leo.

• • •

Who knows what tomorrow will bring? She will be open to anything that presents itself to her.

One night, on her way home from a party on the Lower East Side, she had walked more than a hundred blocks. She'd been in no hurry to get there, to face her punisher. She'd strolled slowly, looking into store windows along the way.

She had passed that sculpture studio where they offered classes — beginner, intermediate and advanced. Maybe she'll take that sculpture class after all. She'd breeze through beginner. Age gives you wisdom and worldly smarts. She'd be intermediate in no time.

She could be a talented sculptress, but more than that even, she could be their muse.

She'll inspire. They'll all be better artists just because she's near them, with her raw, positive energy.

That night, while she was walking home past the studio, she had created, in her mind, the idea of a sculpture. A sculpture of an alien. Not like E.T. but more like one found on The X Files, sculpted in the same form of Venus de Milo. Just a female alien on a pedestal — no arms — frozen and unable to move.

Who needs expensive electronics when Venus de Alien can sit on a shelf in a living room?

Me Goddess. She's going for it, for it all.

Lokanath

THE THOUSAND NAMES OF BALA (THE GODDESS AS AN ADOLESCENT GIRL)

Wearing red clothes, with a *kala* of the moon as Her ornament, effulgent as the rising sun, holding book and rosary, bestowing boons and banishing fears, Bala sits on the Red Lotus. I meditate on Bala.

Pleasing and supremely blissful vermilion One. Ultimate treasure of the path of devotion. Deep left thing. Manifestation of the elements. Shankari. Shiva.

Boon giver of erotic form. Essence. Auspicious sphere of action. Ocean of ultimate bliss. Passionate. Actress. Graceful One. *Kala* of sexual play. The colour of blossom. Dalliance. Absolute. *Kala*.

Suitable essence. Creeper granting all wishes. Eager Goddess. Playing with love's arrow. Truly affectionate. Lovely sweet form.

Effulgent as ten million suns. Cool as ten million moons. Arrow limbed One. Shedding nectar. Means by which heaven is attained.

Gazelle-eyed. Charming. Walking gracefully. Happy and peaceful One. Empress. Queen. Worshipped by Mahendra.

Lady moving in the cosmos. Ultimate mover in the cosmos. With disheveled clothing. Irresistible *shakti*. With tinkling golden anklets.

With breasts like the paradise tree on Mount Meru. Bearing goad and noose as weapons and granting boons. Holding arrows and sugar cane bow in Her two beautiful hands.

Face like the disc of the moon. With a beautiful crest gem, like a little moon. Having a vermilion forehead mark. Her lovely braided hair adorned with flowers.

Rejoicing in a garland of coral tree blossoms. Adorned with a garland of gems. Fond of gold ornaments. Having a beautiful pearl necklace.

Mouth full of tambula. Mind filled with bliss. Pleasing and happy. Essence of passion. Supremely compassionate. Lady of treasure.

An effulgent gem between Her breasts. Intoxicated with wine-essence. *Mantra* that is the essence of *bindu* and *nada*. She is the form of the fourth.

The lovely giver of happiness. Shankari. Fond of blossoms. The universe. Complete. Dweller in the *purna pitha*.

Rajyalakshmi. Shri Lakshmi. Mahalakshmi. Beautiful queen. Santoshi Ma. Excellence. Gold vessel. Light.

All-complete. Supporter of the cosmos. Creatrix. Increaser of strength. Magnificence of all earthly kings. Mother ruling all.

Lotus-eyed One. One gazing long. Clear-eyed One. Flow of love. Taste. 100

Chief One. Essence body. Vermilion essence. Moving gracefully. Colour of pollen. Mad with bliss. Inmost quality. Self of *shakti*.

Eyes full of love. Charming. Goddess of love. Lovely *bhaga*. Beautiful *bhaga*. Taking pleasure. To be enjoyed. Giver of fortune. Lovely. *Bhaga*.

Kala of the bliss between *yoni* and *linga*. Dwelling in the centre of the *bhaga*. Form of *bhaga*. Consisting of *bhaga*. *Bhaga Yantra*. Highest *bhaga*.

Yoni mudra. Kamakala. Essence of *kula* nectar. Fire of the *kula kunda.* Subtle. *Jivatma.* Form of the *linga.* Root cause. Root form. True form of root action. Longing. Lotus bliss. Self dissolved in consciousness. Beneficent.

White and red. Form of *bindu. Yoni* that is the sound of knowledge. Sound of ten million bells. Humming One. The marvelous risen disc of the sun. Dissolved in sound. Completely full. Place of fullness. Many-bodied.

Golden music. Hereditary music. Sound of the drum. Garland of letters. *Siddhi-kala.* Dwelling in the six *chakras.* Playing in the *muladhara. Svadisthana.* Dwelling in the fourth.

Situated in the *manipura.* Loved. Essence of the tortoise *chakra.* Like a flame in the *anahata.* Made of gems.

Vishuddha. Pure sound. Residing in the awakened being. Song. Situated in the *ajna* lotus. Emanatrix. Skillful. Triple circle.

Little moon. Splendid as ten million moons. Shining like ten million suns. Shadow of the ruby-red lotus. Of eternity and joy. Shining.

Auspicious liquor. Deeply beloved. Still and joyful nectar. Charming-limbed One. Rejoicing in union. Sweet nectar.

Seated on a great pedestal. Satisfied. Wild. Beautiful in bearing. Drenched in a shower of nectar. Expanding ocean of redness. Very red. Fond of all that is moist. Wearing innumerable earrings. Removing fear. 200

Excellent oral lore. Encircled by countless flowers and fruit. Dear. Auspicious. Beloved of Shiva. Shankari. Shambhavi. Powerful. Self-created. Beloved of the Self. Partner. One's own. Mother Matrika.

Vowel-being. Refuge. Chaste. Highest being. Origin of wine. Fortunate gladdener. Respected. Devoted to all good fortune.

Lucky. Slender thread. Maiden. Bright as a fragment of a half moon. Beautiful slender creeper. Dear One. Wicked deed. Evil spell.

Fawn's eyes. Excited. Sharp. Intoxicated with nectar. Delighted by liquor. Beauteous as Madeira wine.

Pleased by *kadamba* wine. Handsome. Delighted. Rejoicing in sideways glances. One with slow downward glance. Gazing long and sweetly. Destroyer of the family of demons. Radiant nectar of desire. Suvasini. One with rounded body. One whose breasts are heavy with milk.

Truly beautiful. Her teeth like little pearls. Haloed. Of radiant mouth. Lips like tender shoots. Nose like the tip of a blossom. Forehead shining like gold. Face like the full moon. With a young moon as Her shining diadem.

Lively eyes smeared with orpiment. Ears like blossoming flowers. Each ear like half a leaf. Resembling a new moon. With the sun as a gem in Her diadem.

Wearing golden earrings studded with gems. With coiled and begemmed earrings. Very beautiful cheeks. With a shell-like Neck. Wearing alluring gems.

Wearing a pearl necklace, like the Ganges in flood. Voice like a bird. Limbs extending like many lotus roots. Carrying noose, goad, and bow. With bracelets entwined 'round Her clothes. Adorned with various beautiful jewels. Lotus hands the colour of copper. Her lovely nails shining like gems.

Fingers adorned with jewels. Beautiful lines between Her fingers. Two beautiful breasts like the *mandara* tree. The hair of Her pubic region like a line of serpents. Her deep and womanly navel encircled by the folds of Her waist. Very slender of waist.

Wearing a breastplate for battle. Wearing a beautiful waist cloth. Her buttocks like the brows of an elephant. Her thighs close together like the cheeks of an elephant. Her beautiful legs like bright paradise trees.

With hidden ankles. Her anklets adorned with gems and ringing with a charming sound. Her feet meditated upon by *yogis*. Ocean of wine nectar.

Vermilion ocean. With a vermilion forehead mark. Her hair dishevelled. Perfect nectar. Truly wise. Intelligent. Most beautiful of divinities.

The scarlet rays of a dawn sun. Beloved cow of heaven. Padmini. The essence of nectar. Stream of *rasa*.   300

Beautiful. Ever-present. Giver of boons. Autumnal. Giving true fortune. Dear to Nataraja. Cosmic dancer. Male and female.

Brightly-coloured *yantra*. Web of consciousness. Knowledge vine. Chief thing. Dwelling in the forehead. Five-sectioned. Panchami.

Four-Sectioned.   Tripartite.   Primordial.   Six-Sectioned. Worshipped in the Vedas. Of sixteen parts. The fourth. Supreme *kala*. Shodashi. Goddess of *mantra* and *yantra*. Mount Meru.

Sixteen-lettered One. Three-lettered One. True form. *Bindu*. *Nada*.

Above the letters. Mother of the letters. Great happiness. The Absolute as sound. Consciousness vine. Being with sections. Kameshi. To be seen in dream.

Goddess of dream. Goddess of awakened intelligence. Refuge of the watchful in the waking state. Abode of dream. Deep sleep. Free from idleness. Spring creeper of fragrant white flowers. Madhavi.

Lopamudra. Queen of Kama. Daughter of man. Worshipped by lords of wealth. Shakambhari. Nandi Vidya. Garland of light. Emanating blossoms.

Mahendri. Served in heaven. Oral lore. Refuge of the best *sadhakas*. Chaste. Truly good. *Siddhi* cave.

Lady of the three cities. Worshipped by conquerors of cities. City Devata. Satisfied. Destructrix of obstacles. Without qualities. Worshipped by the celestial cow.

Golden Mother. Lady of hosts. Secret Mother. With beautiful buttocks. Giving birth to all. Liberation. Initiation. Initiated *matrika*.

Mother of *sadhakas*. Mother of *siddhas*. Most powerful wizardess. Deluding the mind. Youthful and intoxicated. Exalted. Her beautiful buttocks swaying slowly.

Dwelling in the red and blue lotus. Smeared with vermilion paste. Adorned with red gems. Wearing a pure red rosary. With a beautiful peacock feather crest. Satisfied by kings. Waving peacock plumes. Perfume diffusing in the cosmos. Earth. Fragrance. Giver of sexual love. Beloved. Giving success in love to those seeking love.

Nandini. Lakshanavati. Devata resorted to by the rishi Vasishta. Devi of Goloka.   400

Protectress of Sri Goloka and all the worlds. Giver of the fruits of sacrifice. Mother of the gods. Giving boons to gods. Wife of Rudra. Auspicious Mother. Wide expanse of the nectar ocean.

Dakshina. Form of sacrifice. True maiden. Rejoicing in resolution. Dwelling in the ocean of milk. Pure *yoni*. Beautiful-eyed. Dwelling in beauty. Truly served. Dissolved in beautiful scents. True in actions. Beautiful Tripura. With beautiful breasts. With the breasts of a young maiden.

Menstruating girl. Showing Her menses. Colourful One. With a bright garland. Liking red. Very red. True form of love-making. Mother of menses and semen. Intent on sex play. Climax.

Cry of orgasm. Self of all love play. Life of the gods. Bliss of *svayambhu* menses. Fond of *svayambhu* menses. Pleased by *svayambhu* menses. Cause of creation of the beautiful *svayambhu* menses. Place of *svayambhu* menses. *Shakti* hole. All love dalliance, Her true and sacred pedestal.

Inner wild woman. Messenger. Artful. Pleased by worship. Kullika. Dwelling in a *yantra*. Dwelling upon a pedestal. With beautiful body. Form of the quintessence. Having all characteristics. Wearing various beautiful jewels. Worshipped with five arrows. Residing in the upper *trikona*. Bala. Kameshvari.

Worshipped by hosts. Worshipped by *kulas*. Lakshmi. Sarasvati. Pleased by spring. Beloved. Having gems on Her breasts.

Bearing a half-moon on Her forehead. Her feet bringing flowers to bloom. Residing in *kalas*. Fond of flowers. Wearing flowers. Deludress of love.

Intoxicated with desire. Mohini. *Kalas* of the moon. Shoshini. Vashini. Rajini. Pleasing. Gracious One. Pusha. Vasha. Charm. Delight. Pleasure. Fortitude. Riddhi. Beneficial to all. With a garland of rays. With parts.

Moon. True shadow. Rising full moon. Satisfied. Full *amrita*. Dwelling in the *yoni yantra*. Residing in the *linga yantra*.

500

Body of Shambhu. *Yogini* of sexual intercourse. Wine goddess. Body of gems. Steady. Dear to seekers.

Self of the king of gems. Giver of dominion and happiness. Granter of desires. *Shakti* of menses and semen. Knower of Shiva's semen. All nectar. Consisting of nectar. Consisting of Shiva and Shakti. Lady.

Dwelling in the bliss of lovemaking. The *matrika* fond of lovemaking. Bliss of the flowers of sexual intercourse. Lovemaking. Expander of *yoga*. State of happiness in sexual intercourse. Served by unified bliss consciousness.

True form of oblation. Giver of success in worship. All one bliss. Supreme. Female form. Fond of lovemaking.

Messenger of knowledge. Accessible knowledge. Origin of knowledge. Abode of Shiva. Consciousness-*kala*. Knowledge with all its parts. True *kula*. Beautiful Self of *kula*.

Four *kalas*. Very subtle lotus girl. Padmini. Supreme being. Dwelling in the play of Hamsa. Shadowy One. Emanatrix of the two parts of Hamsa.

Free from passion. Liberation *kala*. Supreme indweller of *kalas*. Self-situated in Vidya Kala. Dweller in the four *kalas*. Knowledge that brings contentment. Pleased. Light of the Supreme Absolute. *Paramatma*. Dissolved in all things. Fourfold *shakti*.

Diffusion of peace and wisdom. Inner essence of the highest knowledge. She who sees all. Supreme quintessence. Inner *atma* without parts. *Akula*.

Middle Way. Eloquence. Bliss of *atma kala*. Dweller in *kalas*. Swift One. Star. Dissolved in the Shiva *linga*.

Moving for the ultimate good. Delighting in the bliss of the Absolute. Intoxicated with *rasa*. Highest *rasa*. Successful. Fond of success. Uma.

Fond of all castes. Increaser of the bliss of *yogis* and *yoginis*. Bestower of the heroic frame of mind. Celestial One. Giver of true heroism.

Great giver of the heroic mood to Pashus. One whose head is bathed. Queen Shri. The ultimate *matrika* of warriors.

Skilled in sword and missile. Grace. Essence. Enlivening in battle. Victorious. *Yogini*. Pilgrimage. Crusher of great armies. Full.   600

Goddess of wealth. Wealth. Great hoards of treasure. Dwelling in heaps of gems. Jewel. Abiding in necklaces of gems. Maheshi. Worshipped by kings. With hosts. Bearing hosts. Creatrix. Free-loving. Attainable by *yoga*. Mallasena. Female foot soldier. Battle array. Brave in love. Banner. Dwelling in the banner.

Beautiful parasol. Little Mother. Amba. Fragrant. Discipline. The dignity of kings. Of Brahmins and Kshatriyas. Dwelling in sun and moon. Fond of priests. Chaste. Brahmin girl. Multitude of sacrifices.

Supreme wine of the moon. Origin of all. Burning One. Patient. Opposing evil. Bearer of all. Creatrix of all. Origin. Eternity. Gayatri. Attainable by knowledge. Initiated. Giving the wished for goal.

Dwelling in the cosmos like jeweled rays. Life of the universe. Giver of success in the field. Augmenter of all. Little usurer.

Support of *kula*. One who extends Herself beautifully. Mind's delusion. Sanctuary. Pure. Dwelling in the twice-born. Doer of actions. Worshipped in festivals.

Appearing in various guises. Bala. Wanton. Consisting of *kalas*. With beautiful ears. Highest of all. Victorious over difficulties.

Durga. Dwelling in the Vindhya forest. Beloved of the God of Love. Pacifier. Black One. Protectress. Intoxicated with *rasa*.

Appeaser of those fallen from the three rules of conduct. Bestower of complete happiness. Little moon of the cosmic pleasure garden. Giver of happiness to the multitude of *siddhas*. Worshipped by hosts of *yoginis*.

Body of the sixteen *nityas*. Kameshi. Bhagamalini. Nityaklinna. Bherunda. Vahni-Mandala-Vasini. Great goddess of wisdom. Eternal. Shiva's message.

Swift. Beautiful. Daily discipline. Nilapataka. Vijaya. All that is auspicious. Wreath of light.   700

Vichitra. Great and beautiful queen of the three realms. Host of *gurus*. Supreme *guru*. Lady Prakashananda. Form of Shivanandanath. True form of Shaktyanandanath. Consisting of Devyanandanath. Lady Kaulesha Anandanath. Form of the Divyaugha. Lady Samaya Anandanath. Lady Shukla. Kulesha Ananda Nathini.

Body of Klinnanga Ananda. Samaya Ananda Nathini. Veda Ananda Nath. United with the bliss of the Lord.

Body of the Siddha Augha. Body of the highest *guru*. Bliss of the blue sky. Goddess of universal bliss. Bright bliss goddess. Goddess of passion. Primordial lady of the worlds. Primordial playful One. Nandana Ananda Nathini. Body of illumined self. Beloved Goddess.

Self of the Manava Augha Gurus. *Guru* of the *gurus*. Ultimate secret. *Guru shakti*. Fond of those who sing in praise of the *guru*. Bewilderer of the three worlds. All-encompassing and complete.

All-bewildering. Devata of the Eastern Amnaya. Shiva-Shakti. Auspicious power. Dwelling in three Shiva *chakras*. Giver of great fortune. Bestower of all boons. All-protecting. Devata of the Southern Amnaya.

Dwelling in the centre of the sun disc. Devata of the Western Amnaya. Creating and dwelling within the nine *chakras*. Devata of the Northern Amnaya. Worshipped by Kubera. Origin of family. Residing in the exalted Kula Amnaya.

Making and dwelling in the *bindu chakra*. Lady of the central lion throne.

Shri Vidya. Mahalakshmi. Lakshmi. Self of the three Shaktis. Giving All Dominion. Pancha Lakshmi. Eternal truth. Supreme light source. Supreme Shambhavi. Without parts. Matrika. Five sheaths. Swift Goddess.

Parijateshvari. Trikuta. Panchabaneshi. Panchakalpalata. Panchavidya. Source of *amrita*. Wine. Lovely lady. Bounteous nourishment. Cow of plenty. Blessed wisdom. Siddha Lakshmi. Matangi. Bhuvaneshvari. Varahi. Goddess of the five jewels. One who dwells in the letters of *matrika*. Supreme effulgence. In the form of all words. Aindri. Desire.

Independent. Vision of *shakti*. Seed of the sun. Having the body of Brahma. Having the body of Shiva. Having the body of Vishnu. Residing in the wheel of creation. Having the body of the sun. Dissolved in the *chakra* of places. Having the body of Mercury. Mahatripurasundari. True form of *tattva* and *mudra*. Pleasant One.   800

Mudra of cosmic wisdom. Deeply satisfied by ritual. Dwelling in the heart. Divinity of the head. Divinity of crown *chakra*. Absolute. Amorous three-eyed One.

Dwelling in the missile. Four-square. Dwelling at the doors. Dwelling in each door. Anima in the West. Laghima in the North. Mahima in the East. Ishitva, divinity of the Southern Door. Vashitva in the Northwest. Prakamya in the Northeast. Bhukti in the Southeast. Iccha in the Southwest.

Brahmi. Maheshvari. Kaumari. Vaishnavi. Varahi. Aindri. Chamunda. Mahalakshmi. Dwelling in the ten parts.

Kshobhini. Dravini. Divine gesture. Akarshana. Unmadana. Mahankusha. Khechari. Seed of all. *Yoni mudra.*

Dwelling in the *sarvashapura chakra*. Cause of successful *siddhi*. Kamakarshini Shakti. Buddhi Akarshana. Ahankara Karshini. Shabda Akarshana. Sparsha Akarshana. Rupa Akarshana. Rasa Akarshana. Gandha Akarshana. Chitta Akarshana. Dhairya Akarshana. Smritya Akarshana. Bija Akarshana. Amrita Akarshini. Nama Akarshini. Sharira Akarshini Devi. Atma Akarshana. Form of the sixteen vowels. Temple of the flow of nectar. Tripureshi. Form of *siddha*. Dwelling in the sixteen petals.

Queen of the all-agitating *chakra*. Lady of the Guptatara Shaktis. Ananga Kusuma Shakti. Ananga Kati Mekhala. Ananga Madana. Ananga Madanatura. Ananga Rekha. Ananga Vega. Anangankusha. Ananga Malini. *Shakti* of the eight divisions of the alphabet.

Making and dwelling in the eight petals. Shrimat Tripurasundari. Giver of all happiness and dominion. Lady giving great good fortune. Lady of tradition. Cause of all agitation. Causing all to flee. Attractor of all. *Shakti* gladdening all. Crushing *shakti*. Immoveable *shakti*. *Shakti* causing all delusion. *Shakti* causing all subjugation. *Shakti* who gives colour to all and everything. *Shakti* causing awakening. *Shakti* giving the fruit of all desires. *Shakti* giving all wealth. *Shakti* consisting of mantra. *Shakti* causing the dualities to disappear.   900

Siddhi Tripura Vasini. Lady giving all desires to a *sadhaka*. Lady giving the fruit of all actions. Lady of the fourteen-angle *chakra*. Devi giving all *siddhi*. Giver of all prosperity. *Shakti* beloved of all. Cause of all good fortune.

Full of all sexual desire. Liberator from all sorrow. Alleviator of all death. Destructrix of all obstacles. Devi beautiful in all limbs. Giver of all great good fortune.

Tripureshi. Giver of all power. Dwelling in the ten triangles. Lady bestowing all protection. Unborn *yogini*. Knowing all. *Shakti* of all. Giver of all dominion. Devi consisting of all knowledge. Destroyer of all ailments. True form of all support. Destroyer of all evil. Devi made of all bliss. True form of all protection. Mahima Shakti Devi.

Devi giving all. Lady residing in the inner ten angles. Golden maker of garlands. Lady destroying all disease. Mysterious *yogini*. Goddess of speech. Vashini. Devi Kameshvari. Modini. Vimala. Aruna. Jayini. Sarveshvari. Kaulini. Giver of *siddhi* in the eight angles.

Lady who gives all love. Parapararahasya. Dweller in the square and triangle. Self of all dominion. Kameshvari arrow form. Kameshi bow form. Kameshi noose form. Kameshi goad form.

Indra *shakti*. Residing in the sphere of fire. Presiding Devi of Kamagiri. Resting in the lowermost angle of the triangle.

Lady dwelling in the rightmost angle. Vishnu Shakti at *jalandhara*. Residing in the sphere of the sun. Rudra Shakti in the leftmost angle. Brahma Shakti in the sphere of the moon. *Anuragini* dwelling at *purnagiri*. Auspicious lady of the sphere of the triangle. Tripura Atma Maheshvari.

Lady residing in the sphere of all bliss. Secret One who dwells in the *bindu*. Supreme true form of the Absolute. Mahatripurasundari. Dwelling within all *chakras*. Chief of the whole of the *chakras*. Lady of all *chakras*. Lady of all *mantras*. Lady of all wisdom. Lady of all speech. All lords of *yoga*. Undivided lady holding dominion over all *pithas*. Sarva Kameshvari. Lady of all *tattvas* and dominions. *Shakti*. Eyes intoxicated with bliss. Without duality. Womb of dualities.

Unextended in the cosmos. Mahamaya. Extended throughout the cosmos. Dweller in Herself. Supporter of all manifestation in the cosmos. Ultimate bliss beauty. 1,000

Rachel Kann

THE BENT: LILY SUSSES

Dig:
If Honcho made us,
then there is me, Lily,
and there is Honcho, the Creator,
and there is AJ, first man, but second person; second to me,
and then there is Eva, the third, the girly fool
who got used like a tool,
and then Snake Eyes, contemptible tempter,
instigator extraordinaire.

So what I am basically saying is,
if Honcho isn't in a body, then that's not really fazing me.
Right?

I have no frame of reference to know
that I am in a body and Honcho is not.
If Honcho says he made me, who am I to disagree?

I mean, before leaving the Old Neighborhood,
or I should say,
to put more fine a point on it,
until I was unceremoniously chucked out of the whisper-hole,
or really,
let's be honest here,
when Eva swallowed the bait from Snake Eyes,
that's when I first saw other people in bodies.

And to make this all the more annoying,
and confounding,
I am less sure every day that I am not Eva,
and Snake Eyes,
and Honcho,
and even the escape artist — the amazing, disappearing AJ,
because before getting here,

I can't say that I much noticed the whole body thing,
let alone gender.
Gender.

AJ and Eva got the chance to get used to everything
back in the Old Neighborhood,
before heading East.
Thinking, crying, feeling, tasting, touching, smelling, listening,
everything. KissingSpeakingEatingEverything.
Awareness.
On us.
All of us.
You, too.

Pardon me for being the blinder-ripper-offer-du-jour,
but
why do you think you're reading this?
You think that's an accident?
Some random happenstance?
Like Snake Eyes on the corner rolling dice?
What,
ya think that's all arbitrary?

You're still reading.

You have free will,
dontcha?
Maybe you're looking for something.
Maybe all your life you have been.
Maybe you need me as much as I need you.
Maybe I am you.

As I was saying.

As I was saying, Honcho: No Body.
Nobody meaning No Body.
Still Head Honcho, hell yes.
Honcho is as Honcho does.

I have no reason to believe otherwise
when Honcho says I come from Honcho.
I am Honcho.
And you.

If Snake Eyes fed Eva the fruit of knowledge,
ok then,
Honcho,
I am begging, feed me the fruit of haven't-got-a-clue.

Mold me to be a clueless girl-thing.
Let me feast upon blissful oblivion.
Naw, that's a cop out. Scratch that.
But still.

It's not that we didn't have bodies.
It's that we didn't have guile.
We were just being.
Just beings, being.
We were just.

I remember how AJ smelled.
Like good.
Like everything, et cetera.
Like leaves, and warm, and home, and hot,
and how he felt.

It made a lot of sense.
It seemed to.
That's how it felt.
Like tumblers falling inside a lock.
That feeling was a word,
was a way,
was a breath,
an energy,
a symbol.

I'm trying to remember.

Honcho taught me by making me guess,
and it was a secret code.
It was the feeling of inside the whisper-hole.
It was how I got out of the Old Neighborhood —

Because I chanted the magic spell.

Back in the Old Neighborhood,
did AJ always want to be on top?
Yes.
And did I find that wholly unacceptable?
Guilty as charged, your honor.
But was that the only reason why I left?

I'm trying to explain this to you:

Let's say you're at a pizza joint, okay?
Just a regular, old, what-have-you pizza joint.
You are having a slice.
It's good.
Then, say someone comes in and offers you
a free first-class ticket to Rome,
and a place to stay when you get there.
Of course, you decide to go.

Now, is it the pizza that drove you away?
Do you go to Rome to flee the slice you were eating?
This is about the going-toward, not the escaping-from.

I love pizza.

And I love AJ.

He is me.

But a whisper-hole is a whisper-hole,
and maybe there's no comparing anything to that.

That nothingness that is floating.
Not dark or light.
Nothing to say but what it is not.
No-time.
No-place.

Still, there is energy,
something buzzing and electric.
There is vibration.

Halation.
That's when something has a glow around it.
Like on TV.
Like halo-ation. Like an object on TV
that is really bright having a glow around it.
Halation.

There still is something that seems like breath.
Like halations: Inhalation. Exhalation.
The whisper-hole is a thing like that.

Like if AJ was the key inside me,
imagine if I was the whole key inside the whisper-hole.

By the way, that's exactly what I was,
back when I knew the magic word:
The form of a key to the secret door of the universe.

Shoot.

I can't untangle the sticky-web fact of him,
even if the world at large acts like I don't exist,
and AJ and Eva were made that way.
Combined.

I'm ripped from every script, erased from every text.
My pages are burned, buried, drowned, destroyed.
Hidden and invisible.
And still, here I am. I exist.

Poor Eva, fashioned of his rib.
She is him.
Don't think this makes me not love her,
but can't she just be her own person?

For all this hemming and hawing over AJ
and how the sunlight smells when it gets caught in his hair,
I tell you,
what I remember first is Honcho.

I remember Him, like a voice in my head,
only there was no voice and there was no head,
but it was pretty much like having
a conversation in your own head
with someone really smart, and funny, and complimentary.
I remember enjoying this undivided attention
very much.

Honcho, well, Honcho is,
if Honcho is anything —
Cool.
Smooth.
Cool.
Honcho isn't so much a man,
as an entity that wants to be perceived as a man.
At least by me.

Don't ask me why.
Honcho can act so petty sometimes,
with all his guidelines.

Honcho wants me to think of him as a male.
I am not sure what to make of that.
Is this my hang-up or His?
Are we there yet?

Who's the one that thinks you need a magic wand
to create with?

This conversation goes on inside my head,
my consciousness or whatever,
from even before, when there was no head.
Just the halation.
The in and ex of it all.

What's messed up is this:
Like every other guy,
Honcho thinks He was Jim Morrison in a past life,
or you know what I mean. With Honcho,
it's not a past life.
There was no one before Him. Or Her. Him, Her, whatever.
Not reincarnation.
It's just a Jim Morrison skinsuit he jumps into.

This Creator guy,
this all-powerful guy,
the B.M.O.C.,
He appears,
(which isn't right,
'cause it's not with my eyes
that I see Him),
but he looks just like
Jim Morrison.

Honcho, who could be anyone,
or anything,
He wants to be,
including Himself,
whoever that is.
Herself?
Itself?

Honcho, Creator, Lizard King, chooses to appear.
To me.
As the Lizard King.

Dig that.

And the messed up truth is,
after getting chucked out the whisper-hole,
and into this Real World, this New Neighborhood,
I did have little-all-else for options.

Where was I gonna go?
What was I gonna do?
At first, I thought I was gonna die.
And you know I tried.

Then, Eva got me a job with her.
We were working at Enoch's Drug and Discount.
Me and Eva.
Two sisters.
Living in the trailer.
Learning to subsist on
Satinmelt Pasteurized Cheese Food Product and stuff.
It's amazing what a human being can get used to.
Dig?

After a few shifts doing inventory,
I had my very own itchy-hideous polyester frock,
and was cashiering just like Eva.
I was a g.d. drone,
trying to numb away the pain,
dull myself into oblivion,
think less,
feel less.

This world is amazingly helpful with that.

I just wanted to find another whisper-hole.
I needed to talk to Honcho first,
but sometimes, I could hardly even remember that.
He was the language I was forgetting,
so sometimes,
mostly,
and more every day,
I felt just like everyone else on this planet.
I felt that vague, nagging feeling,
like there something I was forgetting,
that word on the tip of my tongue.
What was that word?

Whelp.
That was one thing that came close to the whisper-hole,
even closer than sleeping did,
and it was something AJ could never give me.
I'm guessing he never gave one to Eva neither.

The big O.

Yeah.
I just want to be.
To be full.

In that moment,
I am an instrument.
I am a trumpet, and I am being played with major virtuosity.

Make no mistake,
I know I bring myself to the mountaintop,
but then,
then, at the peak?
The crescendo?
I am not doing at all.
I am so much in my body,
feeling so much inside my body,
that I am out of my body.
I am the empty Transcendesert of my dream-life,
full of stars and black night.
Not in it.
I am it.
Get it?

I am simple waves of vibration.
I am a tube of concentric circles looping,
up and down,
up and down,
through each other,
through each other,
circles of energy up me,
circles of energy down me,
all at the same time,
passing through each other.

My inside is doing that too,
and I am not controlling any of it.
I am just letting the virtuoso play.

I am not speaking metaphorically about this.
I am saying.

I'm saying!

I'm saying that
with nothing else to do in this boring existence,
I have gotten really, really good.
I mean, so good that
I can see through it all.
Someone is there.
Someone familiar.
Someone female.

Men are a steadfast source of disappointment.
Like diss-appointment.
Like getting dissed during your appointment.
Like while having been appointed equal human being,
AJ refusing,
because, say what you want,
there's no way around the fact that
whoever is less invested wins.
The less you put in, the less you have to lose.

I was not built for submission.
Leave that diminutive stuff to Eva.

Man!
What a piece of work is man.

Shakespeare, right?
Shakespeare,
he wrote to the beat of the human heart
to mess with you.

With the rhythm of your listening,
it does.
It casts spells —
magic words,
that are twisted and hidden by men,
yet again.

Like Honcho and his golden ticket,
his tetragrammaton,
his Open Sesame,
his ineffable
name that cannot be spoken.
His secret code.
Man!
Men.

So there's this curse.
Like if you are in a theatre, you can't say the word Macbeth,
unless it's during an actual performance of that specific play.
Only onstage.
In the context of the script.
No kidding.
These dramatists are serious.
You have to say The Scottish Play instead.
And if someone does slip up and say Macbeth,
you have to break the curse by saying,
"Angels and ministers of grace, defend us!"
That's from Hamlet, when his dad's ghost comes to visit.
Ain't that something? Seriously, you tell me, honestly,
is that something, or not?
Magic words and curses and spell-breakers
and Honcho's unpronounceable name, right?

Dig.
So the question remains, in terms of the Macbeth Curse,
who started it? Where'd it come from?
In Macbeth, there are three witches, three weird sisters.
Powerful. Prescient. Without need of men, hence, terrifying.

So these witches, they existed in real life, in the Real World.
That's the theory.
They were real, Real World, New Neighborhood, real.
Forgotten, or more precisely, erased, like me.

And they were none too pleased
with old Willy S. co-opting their
magic words for box office profits.

So I'm just saying, Honcho, head Honcho, who are you?
And whose magic word is it, really?
Maybe a woman's?
Maybe yours?
Maybe you are that woman?
Maybe you stole the truth from yourself?
Maybe I did. Shoot.
Maybe we're all just a bunch of self-plagiarizing
witches with chips on our shoulders.
Righteous chips, but still.
Why this burden?
Why this heaviness of three-dimensional existence?
Stuck in the muck of this time-space continuum?

Basically, I keep coming at it from every angle,
and it adds up to the same thing:
This sense of entitlement.
Honcho and AJ and Snake Eyes
and Shakespeare and Jim Morrison and whatever.
You can all kiss my butt.
What a disappointment.

And yet.

I wake up inside a dream again,
and I'm in the Transcendesert.

I'm just waiting for Honcho,
for the inevitable,
for the predestined.

I may hate it, but he's got the key.

I do love
Honcho.
He is the sensation of trying to taste my own teeth.
He is me.

Kathie Giorgio

FROM GRAVITY, WE ARE FREE

We walk as land—as a solid, living earthquake. All of us Fat Girls. We roil, and we undulate, and we steam. If you look close, you see mountains. If you look closer, you see volcanoes of smolder and depth and flame.

There is an extra layer of Woman upon us. We are Woman, at all of her best. Sensuality is skin upon skin, and we are everlasting skin upon skin. Neck to breasts to stomach to thighs, calves, and ankles. Everywhere. Skin is touching and moving in a constant exorbitant embrace. We are an ocean, rolling ceaselessly over ourselves, rolling ceaselessly over you.

We are inch upon inch, foot upon foot, of high-tempered nerve-endings. We are hypersensitive and mega-aware. Every touch is magnified. Every touch we give is fully loaded.

We are everywhere. You see us sitting on a subway or a park bench, or walking slowly down the street. We appear to sink into the ground with every step. You see us as sad, as having one foot, one knee, one thigh in the grave. You see our bodies as our coffin.

For some of us, that's true. If a Fat Girl is still shrinking from human reprimand, if she is still shying away from her own depths, then she is sad. How hard to be so large and feel so small at the same time! How could such richness be worthless? Why should we want to be shallow? Sheer excess makes us alive and life-seeking and free. We dive into ourselves and then rejoice outwardly, making thin air thick with life and soul and spirit. We are not sinking. We are savoring. There is an extra layer of Woman upon us.

We know how to relish, and we do. We enjoy all that is offered and earthy and real. We feel every motion through our bodies. Those motions are delicious. The earth is at our feet, and the sky is above our heads. The ocean is our heartbeat. From gravity, we are free.

When we are accompanied, we are with those who appreciate us. They understand that the heft of our breasts, each lifted and celebrated in two hands, comes from more than hunger. It comes from desire. The desire to know it all, to feel it all, to embrace and take in and expand. It comes from joy.

Have you heard us sing? Have you heard the full voices that swoop out of full bodies, that climb scales, that fall back and soar again, through stanzas and staffs and serenades? Ours are voices that flood a room.

The voice of Woman. The voice of pure joy. Satisfaction.

We have an extra layer of Woman upon us.

Fat Girls recognize each other from across the room. We recognize each other from across the continent. We pass each other, and we nod, and we know. Our smiles are for us alone.

Can you imagine us all together? See us arm in arm, flesh to flesh, under a moon that is one glorious curve — one full circle, a reflection of all that is light and dark and grounded and floating. The moon calls us out, with the chill of the air. We meet amid songs and exhibition. Our skin glows silver. Our hair flows free. There is a path to the sky and to us. This connection of skin and silk and silver and curves and glory is larger than life. On earth, we are the moon. In the sky, the moon is us — round and fulfilled.

From gravity, we are free.

Moon-soaked, we raise our faces, and we sing. All those voices soar from all those bodies, rustle trees, wave oceans, spark skies. We are round faces atop round bodies. We are round mouths inundating melody, harmony. Round hands slap round knees in rhythm. All of us are rejoicing. We are Rejoice.

We are alive. Everything in us is bounty and burgeon. We are full. We are large. We are lovely. When you look at us, you should never see death — never a foot in a grave, never a body as a coffin. Just life. Life in curve upon curve, in mountain cresting mountain. Life in our touch, our song, our connection to the earth and the sea and the moon.

We are the Fat Girls. We have an extra layer of Woman upon us. We are Woman. From gravity, we are free.

Christopher Connolly

INVITATION

Stop making sense
Just for one day
Just for one life
That's all I ask

Untuck your shirt
Unclasp your hair
Just for one hour
That's all I desire

Run with me in the wilderness
With no compass
Other than our sympathy with rivers
And one another

We can always turn back
To the glowing cities
Their laconic mannequins
Offering pale consolation

We'll take pleasure in
The merciful spray of fire hydrants
Dreaming of other falling waters
Other lives

Christopher Connolly

WHERE ARE YOU?

The poets I want to hear from
Breathe tear gas and barricades
Plastic handcuffs and nonviolent resistance
The difficult bruises of truth's insistence

They kiss passionately in blind alleys at 4 a.m.
Clutching leather jackets
Whirling with desire

They make love in simply furnished flats at sunrise
Their ecstatic sighs
Illuminating entire cities

They embody
The creative fury of strong winds on desolate beaches
The succulent mystery of tropical forests
The compassionate humor of ancient mountains
The supple heat of lava flows

They love the feel of
Foreign tongues
Wild rivers
Smooth flesh
Forest fires

They traverse deserts at night
Conversing with no one but sand and stars

Rod Farmer

AFTER REREADING THE TAO TE CHING

Both the old Taoist philosophers
and the new physicists tell me
time and space are not things
but characteristics of
ceaseless transformation.
In this metaphysics each
phenomenon, each thing,
is not a thing but a unique
impulse in an infinite
temporal flow.
It is these unique impulses,
events, that give us our
meaning of time, and each
of us is an impermanent
energy impulse,
an impulse like a wave
that will flatten into
non-existence.

Should I be
happy or sad that I am one event
in a stream of impermanence
that is more primordial than
the gods we have imagined?

Rod Farmer

NOTHING THERE

I ask for directions
down the road into
an American desert,
The gas station attendant says:
"There ain't nothing out there."
Just the words
I had hoped to hear.

Sumalee Mahanarongchai
with Richard Marranca

THE BALANCE OF COMPASSION

Nowadays, societies around the world seem to be more chaotic and disorderly. Conflict and violence can be found everywhere. People demand their right to exist. Some possess more and more, while natural resources have been scarce, not sufficient to distribute to all. We have to compete in order to get what we desire. High competition brings about fatigue toward oneself and hatred toward others.

As we fight for what we want, confusion and hesitation appear, even in the minds of moral people. We have been taught since we were young to be benevolent. Still, how much mercy can we show, and how can we keep faith in humanity? Should we be hospitable to a depressed gun-holder who is ready to shoot even innocent children? Can we be kind with our competitors? Why do good things that we have done usually end up in vacuity? It seems that the more and more goodness we think of and act upon, the less and less satisfactory are the outcomes that follow. Is virtue meaningful only in an ideal world?

Religious thinkers and philosophers throughout the history of mankind have scrutinized these questions. Prince Siddhãrtha was one who crossed over the confusion. He found the balance between compassion toward all beings and tolerance for seemingly incurable minds. His infinite compassion did not contradict his strict adherence to *dharma*. He was never obeisant to those who committed faults. Why did he insist on helping countless beings be liberated, while the world was full of ignorant and cruel persons? How could he be compassionate to the undeserving and self-centered? How could he preach day and night with a smile, offering friendship at all times? What is the trick behind such a performance? We will explore the truth he discerned.

Unavoidable Truths

What makes Buddhism unique from other religions is Gautama Buddha's discovery of impermanence, the suffering caused by adherence to the impermanence, and the non-substantiality of everything created.

People may imagine permanent and essential things but cannot find them in their relative experiences. The Buddha did not imagine or create any truth. He simply saw and revealed truth with a pure mind.

Impermanence implies change. Change is the natural process that happens to everything without exception. Even our thoughts change moment by moment. Decay is a form of change. Although we do not like it, change continues in societies, in the world at large, and in us.

Suppose that the world were filled with only moral people, or that it was in the best possible condition to satisfy everyone. Still, the world would have to perish and disappear one day.

This is why we should not adhere to the world by imagining it as a fixed and ideal scenario. It is impossible for anyone to freeze the world to his or her expectations. It is suffering to try to do so. Trying to impede worldly change is like trying to stop the flow of the tide. It is a futile endeavor.

Still, to say this does not mean to accept human neglect, to waste the world's resources, or to harm animals freely. Although the world is decaying, we have no right to accelerate its deterioration. We simply cannot expect a steadfast world.

Change makes everything unstable and uncertain. This may seem awful, but actually, it offers the true opportunity for us to determine the course of our lives.

Change and the Law of Action

Since Gautama Buddha realized impermanence, his expectations that the world might be seen as eternally perfect disappeared. With no attachment to his own thought, he performed his duty rigorously. The Buddha taught people day by day, without the feelings of exhaustion, discouragement, or anger.

Is there anything more to his discovery?

In general, people view change with the feeling of dissatisfaction. Change implies an uncertainty that makes us feel vulnerable to the future. Meanwhile, humanity has a mental inclination to want to fix things. We are happy if everything seems to be in our control.

The vision of Gautama Buddha is different. He did not wish for any stable being, event, or thing. He had no desire to control any man. Disappointment and conflict, therefore, could not occur in his mind.

The Buddha once said, "I do not oppose the world, but the world opposes me. The *dharma*-seer will not cause any conflict with anyone in the world."[1]

Not only the world but we also are undergoing transformation. This means that no one can be judged as wholly good or bad. A moral person can turn to be immoral, while a law-breaker can improve his behavior as time passes. If uncertainty is a negative side of change, opportunity is a positive side.

Seeing change is different from thinking of change. If we really see it, we will also see our action and the fruit of the action. The law of action (*karma*) works effectively through the truth of impermanence.

Everyone can determine his or her future through the present action. We think, speak, and do almost constantly. These mental, verbal, and physical actions create new virtuous or unwholesome fruits to strengthen or weaken our minds.

No one is a perpetually good or bad person. A gun-holder who kills innocent people is judged as bad through this particular action. He may be judged differently through subsequent actions. Change gives us an opportunity to redefine our lives.

Change also gives an opportunity for the Buddha not to leave anyone behind. Because goodness or badness is a temporary social judgement, a bad person experiences worldly punishment. Nevertheless, the worldly punishment did not foretell his long-term value. The rotten fruit of a negative action he is experiencing now affects his future destiny just partly. The key to his true value is the continued action that varies moment-by-moment, not a fixed image or social belief toward him.

Because there is not an eternal good or bad person, the Buddha provides his teachings in equanimity. No one is rejected. If an individual is ready to listen to the Buddha, he may accept the doctrine. If not, he may reject it. Acceptance or rejection do not alter the Buddha's intention to help sentient beings become liberated from all kinds of suffering. Gautama Buddha performed his duty with full compassion. In his vast compassion, he also realized impartiality.

Gautama Buddha taught people in a broad range of ways, for he knew that everyone possessed the potential to understand his doctrine and be moral one day. Whether a man was a thief or murderer, he might change and become a very good citizen in the future. Meanwhile, the Buddha did not lift up the already-good persons too high, since he also knew that goodness is not a permanent quality. There are many good individuals who later become prideful and enjoy insulting other people.

The balance of compassion is, therefore, possible through the comprehension of impartiality. Keeping this truth in mind prevents us from losing faith after helping someone who acts badly in return. Impartiality or equanimity of mind protects us from disappointment.

Meanwhile, we can compete with others in order to get what we want, but the competition will be based on fairness. This means that we should do our best. It ought to be our duty to fight for truth and to harm no one.

Truly, we are competing with ourselves. There is no human enemy. The real enemy is our mental defilements. We need not hate our competitors. Competitors are those who urge us to fight against our bad habits. They are teachers rather than enemies.

This may be a reason why the Buddha never felt irritated by attacks from other theorists, teachers, or disciples. We can say that he loved everyone but concerned himself with no one in particular. Although he could not help everybody liberate themselves from suffering, his compassion was full. Although he could not free everyone from the birth-death cycle, his doctrine is still meaningful and applicable. His merciful duty is not suspended in a void. Likewise, if we intend to do something good, even if the outcome turns out to be opposite to our expectation, still the action is meaningful and has some positive values. The virtue can be seen and judged in this actual world.

The Buddha's Prophecy of Men and the World

Since the world and the people in it are changing, growth-and-decline is the common cycle. The Buddha once stated, however, that the world was in the epoch of highest prosperity. People of his time were happy, healthy and long-lived. Human longevity was beyond the comprehension of people nowadays, who mostly live no more than one hundred years. There were only six forms of human sufferings in that age[2]: coldness, warmness, hunger, thirst, excremental need, and urinary need.

Even so, when an oblivious and careless ruler overlooked the custom of giving, the acts of stealing, killing, harming, lying, and various unwholesome deeds followed. When people filled their minds with hatred, greed, and delusion day after day, their lifespans shortened and health weakened. Skins became rough and diseases appeared everywhere.

People were faced with dire situations. There was no set morality accepted among citizens of that earth. Most of them did not respect fathers, mothers, or teachers. They laughed at moral individuals who still took care of their parents and respected seniority. Meanwhile, five-year-old girls were ready to have sexual intercourse[3]; people had sexual relationships like animals. They injured those they disliked.

A small group of people, unable to stand for such behaviors, escaped from society and stayed in the far forest. They did not want to kill or be killed by anyone. They decided to live peacefully and to be moral. When the cycle of deterioration reached its peak and began to decline, the world recovered. The new cycle of prosperity began. These moral people became the ancestors of moral rulers who would keep the cycle of felicity at its peak.

Still, decline would begin again and again. All cycles identify change. The world is changing all the time.

To realize the cycle of the world and of humanity will free us from expectations. Sometimes the world is safe and beautiful, but sometimes it is not. Regardless of our preference, we are not able to fix the world up so as to experience only the positive cycle. Humans will be born in whatever epoch, good or bad, depending on the fruits of their actions.

Still, being born into a chaotic and immoral era need not have only bad effects. We will suffer if we expect too much or judge things according to our own perceptions. We are born, however, to learn the impermanence of things.

Change brings with it the hope to amend human behavior and the opportunity for all beings to awaken.

REFERENCES

[1]Pupphasutta,Suttantapiṭaka,Saṇyuttanikāya,
Khandhavārvagga (Volume 17), Thai Theravāda Tipiṭaka.
Bangkok, Mahāchulālongkorn Buddhist University (1996).

[2]Arakasutta, Suttantapiṭaka, Anguttaranikāya, Sattakanipāta,
(Volume 23).

[3]Cakkavattisutta, Suttantapiṭaka, Dīghanikāya, Paṭikavagga
(Volume 11).

Daniel Ladinsky
AN INTERVIEW WITH DANIEL LADINSKY

Daniel Ladinsky first became known for his unique renderings of the fourteenth century Persian mystic poet Hafiz. He is now internationally recognized for his gifted and accessible renderings of Eastern and Western mystics, as well.

Born and raised in St. Louis, Missouri, Ladinsky lived for six years in western India. There, he worked in a rural clinic that offered free services to the poor, and found a home with the family of Meher Baba.

We caught up with him in Myrtle Beach, via email. It's a blessing to have been able to ask one of our favorite poet-translators about his time spent in India, his writings, and his interior life. It's an even greater joy to share his mystic experiences with you.

Q: What was your life like before living in India, and how did it change when you got there?

A: The idea of God, or maybe you could say the reality of God, dawned on me when I was about twenty, after it had been dormant for some fifteen years.

That is, when I was a child of about five, I was once overwhelmed by a divine presence in thinking I saw God in the sky one day looking down at my brother and me who were out digging a hole to China in the back yard.

That happened to me again when I was twenty, but in a different way. I was on a retreat in the desert near Tucson, Arizona. I was catapulted into a wonderful, wonderful state of consciousness that really remained continuous for about three years. During those three years, while I was in this state that was not in any way chemically sustained, it seemed to me that God's beauty was as accessible as just opening any drawer in my house.

During that period, in my early twenties, the idea started to come to mind to find a living teacher who might in some ways help balance and deepen my experience even more, and that led me to the writings of Meher Baba, and then ultimately to spend some extended time around two men who had been very close to him for their entire lives. They both lived in a place called Meherazad, India, and what I most, most valued and benefited from during my nearly six years in India (off and on over twenty years) was being able to be physically close to these two men. Both of them were pivotal in my coming to work with the poems of Hafiz and the other great poet-saints. It was loving them, these two men, that I feel gave me an essential and needed understanding (at least to some degree) of what Hafiz might have felt for his teacher. Really all of Hafiz's poems were and are very connected to his relationship with his Master, Mohammad Attar, though that relationship seems to be almost completely edited and translated out of the poems that many might attribute to Hafiz.

Q: Was there a pivotal experience for you of spiritual realization and transformation?

A: Several, and I think that is common for anyone who is making some sincere effort on the path or who has the great fortune to get personally connected to a real saint or Master.

I want to create a little foundation for what I will say, by sharing some aspect of spirituality, or Masters if you will, that has long intrigued me. That is the aspect of Knowledge, complete Knowing. I mean, if there is a God who is omniscient and omnipresent, then it seems a reasonable deduction to believe that if a soul were truly one with God, then they would share that experience. It is something so, so, so extraordinary to my mind, that any apparently normal looking human being could truly share that Knowledge, or to be honest, that such Knowledge even exists. It just blows my little brain away.

Back in the 1930's a very interesting, intellectual, and accomplished British man by the name of Charles Purdom met Meher Baba, and then went on to write one of the most down-to-earth books about Meher Baba that I have read. It is called *The God Man*. Purdom spent time with Meher Baba off and on over the years, and during one of Purdom's stays with Baba in India, in 1954, Baba casually remarked to Purdom, "Dear Charles, can anyone imagine how I am here in front of you — and simultaneously everywhere! Can anyone really imagine that? Can you?"

Well, as extraordinary as it may seem, I think I might have spent time with someone who also had that experience (was omnipresent). At least he seemed to, and I really checked that out the best I could. People just called this man Eruch. He first met Baba when he was very young. He joined Baba when he was about nineteen and then became the person who most spoke for Meher Baba, as Meher Baba was silent for forty-four years of his life.

I guess I would have to say that I more than just met Eruch. I spent time with him off and on over twenty years. For six of those years, I saw him on a regular basis and then even lived very close to him for two years. He used to walk almost every morning, starting out while it was still dark, sometimes. On hundreds of occasions I walked with him for miles in the morning, and very often just he and I. He, at times, seemed so powerful to me, or he had such an internal blaze constantly going on within him, that I would walk behind him twenty or thirty feet. I am a somewhat shy and reclusive person, and even though he was the person I clearly most loved on earth, I still felt nervous being around him at times. Also, inherent in being physically close to him was to have him work on me as it were, or maybe to have me (unconsciously) be a part of his work. Either way, that work was very hard, almost impossible for me to bear at times.

On only two occasions when I was walking behind him, that I can remember, did he ever turn around and speak to me. One occasion was this: He most always walked East in the morning, and as I said, we would sometimes leave while it was still dark. So, we are walking, and we are just coming out of a beautiful grove of huge trees, and not far from the grove of trees are some ancient-looking hills, and the sun is just now rising over them. There's something about the just coming out of these trees and seeing the sun just coming up over these remarkable hills and having this profound man some twenty feet in front of me. I almost swoon from the exquisiteness of the beauty all around me. And I get the thought—This is the most remarkable sunrise I will ever see. Just as I get that thought, he turns around and rather playfully shouts, "It is just a blemish on the Beloved's face."

I remember one of my first real meetings with Eruch, in 1978. I was sitting with him in a room with several other people, maybe twenty or thirty. He was seated on the floor where he liked to sit, but he could have sat as naturally on some throne, and I think it would have been the same to him. So, there were some twenty or thirty of us sitting around him. I started to look at him and feel with a tremendous, tremendous certainty—that this man is more me than I am. I was shocked by that feeling, but it seemed one of the greatest truths I had ever personally come across.

Then one more little story, the last. So, he and I are walking again, and we get to a place where he would most always stop for a minute or two. It looked out over a lake. This was also a juncture of a sort, where a mile-long private road met up with a charming, old, paved, rural India road, and where they had a bus stop. I noticed that he liked to interact with strangers or animals that would sometimes be there. This one day we are there, alone, and whenever he would stop I would walk up to his side. So, we are standing there in silence as we most often did, and then he speaks.

He says, "Danny, I hope you don't die without Knowing, really Knowing; but that would take super-human effort on your part. It is the ultimate human duty, the ultimate act of service—to Know."

Real Knowing—gosh. I often feel like one loaded monkey with all the stuff that can go on around these books, and in my personal life at times. I feel like I am lucky not to just fall out of the tree I cling to.

I do hope to, at least someday, try—really try to penetrate into the essence of all being. I really have not yet. I have been playing hooky. All that seems so far, so far beyond me.

At least I feel I have met someone who did, who really Knew. He has changed my life forever.

On one of the last times I saw Eruch, he gave me his short bamboo walking stick that he had carried whenever we walked and that he had had for decades. I have that laying across my computer as I write now. It was there for the past some thousand Hafiz renderings I did over the last year for a new book I just turned in to Penguin called, *A Year with Hafiz.* Some three hundred of those new poems will be there.

I think his walking stick helped a lot. Some of his Knowing and Beauty got into some of those poems, I bet, by God's grace.

Q: Do any of Meher Baba's teachings in particular stand out in your mind today?

A: I think Meher Baba's spiritual status is such that even Rumi and Hafiz could say Meher Baba is the very root of them, as they could say about Muhammad or Jesus or Krishna or Buddha.

I have been hanging out with Meher Baba, the best I can, for forty years now. I think he is the very root of all I do. I don't often like to look at it (for that just seems too precious), but if I do, I can see a profound intimacy between us.

To answer your question more directly now, yes. There is a two-sentence statement of Meher Baba's that I came across when I first started to tango with him, as it were, that has always stuck with me. Those two sentences are: "To penetrate into the essence of all being and significance, and to release the fragrance of that inner attainment for the guidance and benefit of others, by expressing in the world of forms truth, love, purity, and beauty—This is the sole game which has any intrinsic and absolute worth. All other happenings, incidents, and attainments can, in themselves, have no lasting importance."

Q: Do you resonate particularly with the lives of any of the saints whose writings you've translated?

A: Well, I think the reason so many of us are attracted to the lives of the great saints and their writings is because they can still be true teachers and guides to us. They can tell us of experiences to come and help us with experiences we are having. They can help us make greater sense of the inner and outer world at crucial junctures.

Q: What's a day in the life of Daniel Ladinsky?

A: Well, for the last sixteen years I have been consumed with the poetry work. I mean really consumed, like having gone through a three-year period, not too far back, where I literally averaged about seventy hours a week, every week, for three years. I used to have one of the top literary agents in America representing me. He was the former publisher of Harper San Francisco. He went back to publishing about four years ago. Since then, I have been representing myself. This means that all the business stuff surrounding these books, which is extensive, my part-time assistant and I now try to handle the best we can. Sometimes, contract processes with Penguin and other licensing agreements will go on for months. Sometimes, even years. Poetry and legal contracts are opposites in many ways, I feel, but I do what I can with them.

I just want to try to milk myself of every possible little drop of hopeful poetry that might someday be of value to someone, but I am getting tired now and having some health stuff going on. A sixty-year-old body seems to start picking up some dents — aches — in it that are harder to get out. I am starting to spend more time at the wilderness farm I have in the Ozarks and looking forward to retiring there, if the moon does not fall on me one night while we are smooching.

Q: What are your personal spiritual beliefs and practices?

A: I think I have and do at times experience something that even if an atheist were to experience it, that experience would be called God, seeing and feeling God. I also think that all so-called spiritual practices are only valued for their ability to help one to enter the Buddha's mind, the Sun's heart, God's arms, Existence's soul. To know the Truth, or whatever you might want to call it.

It seems at times that my spirit hands can touch all they would ever want to touch. Maybe at some point I hope to be able to go ever more deeply into a realm that others live in all the time. For now, what little spiritual (if you will) work I might have with these books, keeps me very focused on writing, and going about—and often suffering with—the natural and sometimes complex time-involvements that one has to go through to get things done in the common world.

Some lines from a Hafiz poem in *The Gift* comes to mind to your question. Those lines go:

> *Don't die again with that Holy Ruby mine inside*
> *still unclaimed, when you could be*
> *swinging a golden pick with each step.*

What Hafiz (or my rendering of him) is talking about in that poem may not be clear to everyone reading it. The poem, to me, is talking about saying the name of God silently on each step. The name of God, or the name of the Beloved, that might most appeal to one personally. I guess this is by far my most constant spiritual practice. I have been doing this for years and years.

I remember once reading one of the few documented statements of Sai Baba of Shirdi (who became famous around a hundred years ago), who said (slightly rendered here), if it becomes natural for one to say—silently—the name of their Beloved on each chew of food, then soon God will not be able to resist you. Well, that little exercise is now a very natural part of my life. I worked that into the mix a long time ago. Sometimes, I like to meditate in a formal way, but always alone. It seems there is a kind of trap-door at the top of my head and, if I even just slightly concentrate on that, I can at times experience splendor beyond my belief.

Maybe I am getting cuter in God's eyes. I don't know. I think the reality is we are all absolute knock-outs to God, and that He/She/It is reaching for us with all of God's might. That split second of His pulling us up into His arms (or better yet—us knowing we are already there—and have always been there) is what we might call separation, or suffering, and our longing.

Union I think is a shoo-in, the greatest of certainties. I think it is a very naïve and false notion to think one ever has to do anything to earn Union: I feel our very being is our ticket to the Holy. I would say every single poem of Hafiz is really about helping one to know that—our sublime worth—and to drop the knife that most so often use upon their tender self and others. That above line comes from a very short story I will tell that goes like this:

Once a young woman came to Hafiz and asked, "What is the sign of someone knowing God?"

Hafiz became very quiet, looked deep into the young woman's eyes, and held her hand, then replied, "My dear, they have dropped the knife. The one who knows God has dropped the cruel knife that most so often use upon their tender self and others."

Q: Is there a poem of his you've translated that is especially close to your heart?

A: Depending on my mood any given hour, and I surely and still go through many moods in a day, I think I could open one of my books to maybe two hundred different poems and sincerely be touched by it. I'd probably even think it was relevant, and might even sincerely think to myself: Gosh, I wish I could be a part of writing something like that. Then, it turns out, this little loaded monkey was. All to say there is hope for every writer who puts their heart into the pen and prays for help.

Q: What advice would you give to poets seeking to express their relationship with God?

A: For me, what I feel was the biggest help was praying like hell for help, and making a deeper connection at times by meditating. I think there are supervening forces in existence that cannot resist the desires of a pure heart. A heart deeply wanting to help aligns itself with the Unseen, and the Unseen is a vast, infinite treasury. If one sincerely gets involved with art as a way to perhaps benefit others, I think the angels chip in and break open their piggy banks.

One's motives must remain very sincere, though. I think sometimes fame or money can make the angels shy of one, make them withhold their investment as it were.

I am just speaking of angels in a metaphoric way. I have never seen one, but there is a lot I have yet to see.

There is a beautiful line from the Prophet Muhammad about poetry and art (really), which goes:

> *There are treasuries beneath the throne*
> *the keys to which are the tongues of poets.*

So then, the question, you might say, really becomes how to become a poet or an artist. Well, to be frank, I think this is most always bestowed by a saint upon someone they like, or are closely connected to. I think this may be very true: that all of the historic greats who have made the most significant contributions to science, politics, religion, and art have all been souls who were deeply touched—inspired—by their connection with God or some living saint or Master. Surely that is the case with Rumi and Hafiz. I feel at times Hafiz lets me be a kind of footstool for him in this world, or some kind of packhorse who does the dirty work of getting contracts signed and things like that, and proofreading. Boy am I lousy at that.

Q: How do you experience God, or the relationship with the Beloved?

A: I will answer that via a dream that I had some thirty years ago, but that I feel still very much affects my life and my literary work.

In the dream I found myself in a room with Meher Baba. He was seated some ten feet from me and looked very happy to see me. Looking at him gave me the feeling there is really no-holds-barred in this God stuff, and that really, anything goes. I took one step back, revved up all my little engines the best I could, and then ran full speed toward Baba and dove into his stomach.

Once inside, I felt I had entered God. I felt like every sun in creation was just a tiny part of my own light and the light that every creature will someday come to know. I also realized in a second that Danny, the conventional me, never ever possibly could have existed, and that any future thoughts, ideas of an individual self, really could never ever have anything to do with the Truth of who I and everyone or everything really is.

At some point in being inside of God and feeling a Oneness with Him, I felt Baba reach in and pick me up by an ankle. He lifted me out and then dropped me into this world again. Ouch! So here I am—feeling marooned big time, at times, and appearing to appear to many.

I am not really here—and neither are you. We are all really the source of all life and existence. We are just waiting in line to realize that we were never, ever anything but God. Someday we will cease to be duped. The ouch will end.

Q: Please feel free to share with us anything else you'd like.

A: Saadi was considered a Master on the level that Rumi and Hafiz and Kabir were. He is also buried in Shiraz, where Hafiz is, and died a few decades before Hafiz was born.

There is something Saadi said, and this is very close to a literal translation that seems appropriate after saying so much here. Saadi says, "It is wonderful to recite poems and give little talks and discourses, but always wrap it up before someone gets bored."

So, I hope the poems that end this don't make you yawn too much. And I hope they share a big hug with you the best words' arms can.

*This poem is from A Year With Hafiz: Daily Contemplations and is
one of my very favorites in that book. I feel this particular poem distills
the remarkable relationship that can go on between a student and a
teacher — on the various levels within that wonderful dynamic.*

So That You Can Plant More Wheat

I would like to remove some rocks from your field so
that you can plant more wheat.

And those hills I see that are part of you, I have
some trees in mind for them and flowering grasses

so that you won't fear or erode when the elements
pour.

Are we not lovers? Cannot I speak to you like this?

Do I need to ask your permission to hitch up my ox
and sing to him as I improve your vast terrain?

The title to your heart came to my office. In looking
at it a great interest in your soul developed.

So, I would like to remove some stones from your
life so that an orchard you can grow,

and the world will come, the world will then come
to know your talents . . . and taste your riches.

Excerpted from *A Year with Hafiz: Daily Contemplations* by Daniel
Ladinsky (Penguin, 2010).

One of my favorite poems in The Purity of Desire: 100 Poems of Rumi is titled "The Body Is Like Mary." I find this poem remarkably complete, and it has an intriguing statement about art in it.

THE BODY IS LIKE MARY

The body is like Mary, and each of us has a Jesus
 inside.

Who is not in labor, holy labor? Every creature is.
See the value of true art, when the earth or a soul
is in the mood to create beauty,

for the witness might then for a moment know, beyond
any doubt, that God is really there within

so innocently drawing life from us with His umbilical
universe/infinite existence,

though also needing to be born. Yes, God also needs to
be born,

birth from a hand's loving touch, birth from a song
breathing life into this world.

The body is like Mary and each of us, each of us has
a Christ within.

Excerpted from *The Purity of Desire: 100 Poems of Rumi* by Daniel
Ladinsky (Penguin, 2010).

And here are two more short ones, in case anyone is in the mood for more verse.

Nothing Like a Yesterday

When was the last time you felt complete,
so complete, nothing dared approach you?

Nothing like a yesterday, or a tomorrow.
Nothing that could speak.

Nothing that could ever point to anything
that would ever need to be done.

Nothing that could not do anything . . . but
adore you.

Excerpted from *A Year with Hafiz: Daily Contemplations* by Daniel Ladinsky (Penguin, 2010)

Be Like That Cat

Be like that cat, so alive after a mouse,
never questioning or toying half-bored,
with there being only God touching your
paw.

Excerpted from *The Purity of Desire: 100 Poems of Rumi* by Daniel Ladinsky (Penguin 2010).

ACOMA PUEBLO

Susanne von Schroeder

Hugh Fox

Rebirthing Without Having To Die

The house out in Michigan off Babcock (dirt) Road, close to nowhere but corn farms and deer-and-grouse haven forests, had belonged to his father, and before him his mother's father, five sisters, one brother, and one sister in Boston (a pathology professor at Harvard). All the rest were dead (cancer, car accidents, his brother in the WWII army). His kids — in Brazil (one), Boston (two), New Hampshire (one), and one in Ann Arbor, about two hours away — came to visit him once in a while, but always said, "The house needs work. I know you don't have much professor-pension, but to stay overnight, especially in the winter..."

His wife had been dead (more cancer) for five years. He was two months away from his eighty-first birthday. OK, it was now mid-December, and there were enough potatoes (sweet and white), chickens, eggs, cans of vegetable soup, powdered milk, carrots, apples, bottles of juice and Irish Cream liqueur, canned sauerkraut, steak-chunk, oats, sugar, powdered coffee, beer, and canned beets to last all winter.

At first hating it, he shoveled the driveway. He walked Ludwig Van, his poodle, through the snow. He worried about the roof's collapsing under the snow build-up, but it had lasted for a century and a half and...

He made calls to the kids once a week, to old friends in East Lansing, where he had taught English for thirty years, and to old poet friends in Sunnyvale and West L.A., and received emails every day from Glenna out in Carpinteria, a poet pal for fifty years. There was WKAR, classical music twenty-four hours a day (except for the news) and cable TV, and you never knew what you'd find out about the Knights Templar and ancient Egyptian tombs. He watched films like *The Bride Wore Black*, and after he'd seen that one night (by accident), he'd checked Moreau out on an Internet search and found fifty pictures, including one of her at eighty-one. She still radiated magic.

"Waddaya say we hill and swamp it a little today!" he tells Ludwig Van, and Ludwig Van squeals, "OK."

He puts a heavy dog blanket on him. There are three inches of snow on the ground from last night. He wears two sweaters and a heavy coat, heads out the back door, down into ex-cat-tailed now-frozen swamp, up a hill that reminds him of (*The Country Diary of an Edwardian Lady*) ancient England, gets a little fatigued, worries 1.5 on a scale of 10 about his heart, but reaches the river. He walks into the evergreen forest, no longer cold, and adjusts to it like a grizzly bear. The trees and the birds (and one deer quickly escaping from his path) wordlessly tell him, *In the beginning was my talking to you, before you were, without words. Just listen to presence. I am here.*

Hugh Fox

PACE

We finish our sushi — *akagi* rolls,
shrimp and Japanese (Sapporo) beer —
in half an hour. Martha, one hour and
a half later, is still playing around with her
rice and shrimp. When I complain, "The
moon is going down," she purrs, "How
do you think I got to one hundred and
two point five? By being in a rush?"

Ayaz Daryl Nielsen

ASKING MY GRANDFATHER

asking my grandfather
about spirit as we rest
in the wood stove's warmth
his reply — "a desk and
a path through the forest"

Greg Moglia

AND I DIDN'T COMPLETELY SHUT THE CAR DOOR

And the car battery went dead
And I had gone to the movie alone
A movie called *The Edge of Heaven*
Where a son never quite connects with a father
And I come out of the theatre and see my door a bit ajar
And I call AAA and they're in St. Louis and
I'm in New York
They take my message
But it is Saturday night — peak accident time
And they say it will be a wait
And I say okay, and I get hungry
Go for a potato knish just before the snack bar closes
And before I finish I get heartburn
And AAA calls back and says they need to get a
Different station
And they say he can come within the
Next hour
And then it's 2 a.m. and I am alone
The only car left in the lot
And I think how last month
a guy was shot here

And I cough—my air conditioner cold kicking in
And I feel it in my lungs
And a second later an acid reflux burp arrives
And I think I could die here
It wouldn't be the right place, the right time
I'm owed that much
A life of "never miss a day" teaching
I should get a good death
But what exactly would that be?
No such thing as a good death
Okay, but there are enough lousy ones
So let me have one that's a bit better
And I think of Brando in *The Godfather*
Playing with his grandson
Yeah, I can go for that
My guy Jarrett on my lap
Me reading Dr. Seuss's *Hop on Pop*
The last words I hear—his first words
To me about me
"Papa, Papa"

Barbara Fleck-Paladino

MARRIAGE OF HALF-EMPTY TO HALF-FULL

I.

First, you go and marry your father. Spouse One—he's a bully. Finally, through fortuitous stupidity, you get to leave. Even your actual father greets your news with a hearty "Mazel Tov!"

When—second chance—though Spouse Two is again a he, you marry your mother. Your mom and Spouse Two are fond of each other, as if each recognizes something in the other.

Only after Mom's long gone and Spouse Two is longer around does it dawn. The unhappy half-emptiness in him. The sad wistfulness of her.

Your bully dad, in between being a great guy, would be mean and rage at his wife. You'd let him, because then he wasn't putting you down. You wish now you'd called him on it. The fact is, even when he was criticizing any of you, he was your Dear-Old. Isn't there that no-matter-what daughter-father thing operating?

So all this is here, and now there's your Near-Lifelong to untangle and untether.

Original bully and original depressive?

They passed on, but passed it on. They live in us, in the acts of dysfunction we now perform.

In this incarnation, not only have you married your mother, but you've become your father. You hear yourself. You hear the cruel nastiness leaping out of your mouth. Why are you like this?

You see hurt in Spouse Two's eyes.

Dear-Old-Dad, in his time, would start to feel guilty, as do you in yours.

You vow to be more empathic. You try to feel what Amore's feeling. You try to remember being depressed. You recall Mom going through a rocky menopause. Sitting in the armchair, she was oblivious to anything but her mystery stories.

Yet now — you can't help it. That attitude of Amore's smacks of giving up. It's far too familiar for your comfort. How could one live like that?

Still, he does as she did. He doesn't engage. What waste.

Further, Spouse Two has of late taken to not answering you. If anything courts venomous rise out of a person, hasn't talking to a wall got to be it?

Now you know what that saying feels like.

You talk.

He's the wall.

Sometimes he treats you as if you are the wall, as if you don't breathe, live, love, seethe.

Did you sign on for either side of wall-dom? You can't remember doing that when you said, "I do."

But watch yourself becoming enraged. It's a trigger in you that Mister Wall activates, just by doing nothing.

Want to know how a fool feels? (You could ask Dad, but he is no longer. Still, it's unavoidable — remembering him fit to be tied, apoplectic over his wife's remoteness.)

There's something both superior and pathetic about Amore's (and in her time, Mom's) non-entry into the down and dirty fray of everyday living.

Meanwhile, you entrap yourself in childish tantrum.

You've tried answering his not answering with your own non-answering. Let him know how that feels.

He hardly notices.

So it was with your models, Mom and Dad.

He would rant and carry on.

She would non-respond.

What a pair.

The situation raises hackles. (What are hackles? Those things on the back of a Stegosaurus? Plates? Prehistoric.) Hackles feel like shackles. Shackles chain you down.

Empathy. That's the ticket. You try to put yourself in his place, even the tiniest bit. You remember how your heart went out to your mom as you grew, even while the child you were had no insights as to what was operating in her.

Nowadays, with Amore, do you really want to know?

It's like being in mucilage. Gluey.

In resin. Suspended.

Paralyzed.

You want to get out. It's not a comfortable skin, his, even if it is a thinner sort. (That part you don't mind.)

But it constricts.

There's little sun.

Less laughing.

There's that half-empty from him.

That almost physical ouch.

There's more often the "no" from him. (Non-empathy you insists on the "yes.")

"Well, it's not so good a day," he says. (When non-empathy Dad-You knows, "What's the matter with you? It's a gorgeous one.")

There is an achiness of the bones from him. Inside out. Outside in. (Non-empathy you is feeling no pain except the referred pain of the Miserable One.)

Is there a solution?

Doubtful.

If you didn't live with Amore day in, day out, observing no overt proof of what he feels, you might be able to sympathize

But there's nothing to see. Seeing. Is it not believing?

You don't want to think you're so thoughtless as to doubt it's reality to him, but it makes you mad. (In both the angered and the crazed senses of the word.)

Seeing your distress, every so often (he is, under all the layers, the best of good guys), Amore says he'll keep trying.

He forgets.

He lapses into the dour.

I suppose if I had to be in his skin, I'd be doing all I could to shed it. To break free.

Would I want to go away?

No.

Should I just be content? Leave it at that? He live his life? Me mine?

Leave him at him? Me at me?

Is this a marriage of half-empty to half-full?

What is its totality?
The tally?
Half what?
Where in the cup is the empty?
Where the full?
Up top?
Down below?

I get distracted by the image. I can't picture it. Gravity always throws in a monkey wrench.

What is it half-empty of? And of what half-full?

What about a cup all empty?

Better — or too greedy? — a cup all-full?

That's the ticket. What about that then?

I try to be more sympathetic. (Since empathy hasn't seemed all that successful.)

I have to take his depression on faith, and faith I'm not good at. If only he would answer when I speak to him.

I ask how it feels to be him.

He won't tell. He prevaricates, as if afraid I'll be so alarmed I'll — what?

Is he embarrassed to admit how unwanted he feels? (His mom was the most adoring of mothers. Nothing was too good for her firstborn boy.)

Does he feel as if he doesn't deserve?

How can he believe that? Of all people. So talented. Smart. He was the prince, growing up. At least, so they say. Have you to believe he's psychically malingering? Being coy? Kidding? Delusional?

(You know how frustrated Dear-Old must have felt about your mom, who was also bright, but didn't fulfill herself. How pulled were your allegiances between the two.)

A whole lifetime of Amore tying himself in knots? Agonizing? Being dark? Is it chemical?

But then what about the other, the shall-we-say arrogant, strand? The perfectionist facet? It's as if, deep down, Amore knows that he deserves all. Nobody deserves royal treatment so much as he, and his depressed veneer is nothing other than his version of being really pissed at how we plebeians treat him.

LALITAMBA

Off his antidepressant, anger surfaces. This gentle, retreating fellow, he fears his own internal Vesuvius and thus clamps himself down.

He's way too patrician to erupt. It's unsightly, and so he lets me do the dirty work. He assigns me that nasty role.

Ought I just let it, let him, be?

For better?

For worse?

II.

My daydream:

It is his birthday.

I greet him with kisses,

take him to breakfast,

to lunch,

to dinner.

Each meal surpasses the one that came before.

(This actually—don't ask how—maybe mutual fatigue at butting psyches?—comes to pass.)

I ply.

I shower him with presents.

I appreciate.

On this day, he smiles. He is lovely in how he behaves to me. He answers every utterance, especially my most inane.

He is grateful: To me. For me. He actually seems to like me. (This newer non-nudge version of me is trying, too.)

There's kissing and hugging.

Nobody is channeling anyone. Nobody's mother or father — dead, alive, or figment—is looking over anyone's shoulder.

And this most elegant of days—best-behaved on both sides—morphs into the quotidien.

Half-full overfloods half-empty,

filling and pouring forth,

until—Who can say how? Who can say why?—our cup runneth over.

Call that a marriage?
Why not?

End (Who knows?)

Barbara Fleck-Paladino

HAPPINESS FOREVER?

what's the secret to happiness together?
yes dear yes dear yes dear yes
listen for silence where you can find it
listen to each other, is that not best?

yes dear yes dear yes dear yes
listen for birds, their tiniest chitter
listen to each other, avoid getting bitter
listen to what's not said; therein lies abundance

listen for the birds, their teensiest chitter
cherish each other, yes that old cliché
listen to what's not said; let honesty matter
clichés come in handy, they're with us for reasons

cherish your here-ness, your now-ness, your seasons
listen for stillness in all forms of weather
it's precious, it's rare, it tells you what's needed
these are some inklings toward happiness together.

Daniel Stolar

THE SACRED AND THE MUNDANE

My wife, Lauren, has just given birth to our second child, to our second baby girl. Anna is her name. I sit in our recovery room in Prentice Women's Hospital in downtown Chicago, and I keep thinking that I don't have the words to explain the happiness I feel.

Why? I keep asking myself. *Why do I feel so full of joy?*

On one hand, the answer is self-evident: My wife has just given birth to a healthy baby girl. Exactly what about this, though, makes me so deliriously happy?

Anna is eight pounds of mush. She can barely be called human at this point. She can't focus her eyes or hold up her head. She can't manage so much as a smile. She certainly doesn't have any personality to speak of.

What if, in the chaos of the ten people bustling about between my wife's spread legs, someone had pulled a switcheroo? I certainly wouldn't have known the difference. At what point does one cross the can't-switch-my-baby-for-another threshold?

Lauren would claim that it is immediate, that a bond has formed while Anna was inside of her and that she would know if a different baby were put on her chest.

I'm not going to try to change my wife's mind. At twenty-four hours, though, I walk into the nursery, see a baby crying in a mobile bassinet, and for a long moment, I mistakenly think it's Anna.

Can it really be love if the object of your love is nearly interchangeable?

As far as the ledger of life is concerned, I'm not at all convinced that children come down on the positive side, anyway. Have I brought my parents more moments of joy in their lives than torment? For my mom, I would say yes, but she died relatively young. For my father, it would be a toss-up. There have been entire years, perhaps even a decade, that would go down on the minus side of the balance.

In my case, preliminary reckoning is not encouraging. I've traded "The Daily Show," "Sportscenter," a good night's sleep, my morning coffee, the *New York Times* "Op-Ed" page, and a run on the lake for a night of no more than one hour of uninterrupted sleep on a three-quarter length loveseat and more than a little contact with bodily fluids that aren't my own. I've traded an attractive woman who enjoyed sleeping with me for a woman who will be physically incapable of sex for several weeks and, even then, I know from experience, far less inclined for more than a year.

What do I have to show for these lopsided trades? Anna is an entirely unresponsive eight pounds of crying, burping, sucking, mush. I jiggle her in my arms as I walk around our tiny recovery room. It has a view of Lake Michigan that I'd never be able to afford if it weren't on Blue Cross Blue Shield.

I know no lullabies. All I can summon are commercial jingles from my youth.

As I bounce Anna on my shoulder and pace mini laps around our hospital room trying to calm her, I coo into her ear: "Mounds Almond Joy's got nuts. Mounds don't. BE-CAWWWZ, sometimes you feel like a nut. Sometimes you don't."

Or, more appropriately, perhaps: "Watch it wiggle, watch it jiggle. Serve Jell-O brand gelatin, and serve some fun."

For those two days in the hospital, time takes on a different dimension. Sixty minutes is just an hour in adult time, but at one point, it is Anna's whole life. Only an hour later, it is half of her life. This strikes me in my sleep-deprived, adrenaline-filled state as terribly profound. Even the next morning, an hour passes, and it's more than five percent of Anna's life.

Anna sleeps cradled in Lauren's arms or against her chest, nursing intermittently, or for a few wonderful stretches on my chest. We rarely use the Plexiglass bassinet.

After two days, one of us has been physically holding Anna for more than 90% of her life — probably closer to 95% or 98%. Imagine, 98% of your life cradled by a human being who — for whatever reason — loves you. From the moment we put her in the carseat to take her home, that will never be true again. The percentage of her life spent being held will begin its long, irrevocable decline, only to be interrupted by a slight upward turn during the beginning of a new romance.

Before we had our first baby, Callie, four years ago, it never occurred to me how much loss is involved in raising a child. I'm not talking about the obvious — losing time alone, losing sleep, losing movies and bars and pocket money and adult conversation. I'm talking about the child herself.

Every day, you lose a little bit of the baby that was your newborn. One of Callie's first words was Ee-oh. She said this for Carlito, our bumbling and mostly blind pit-bull mutt. For some reason, as a toddler, Callie loved that dog, who would often knock her down. For months, "Where Ee-oh" were the words with which she got out of bed in the morning. Then one day, she said his full name. Carlito. It was months before Lauren and I realized that we'd never hear the word "Ee-oh" again.

Somehow, I think loss, that endless miniature mourning, is intimately connected to the irrational joy I feel holding little Anna. I know that this moment, and this moment, and this moment, I will never have again with her. It's true of each moment of our everyday life, of course, but your own baby puts it into stark relief.

Anna roots blindly around my cheekbone with her lips. It's an instinctual, animal-like movement that disappears forever a couple of months after birth.

As I jiggle her and sing the Dr. Pepper jingle, I am as happy as I've ever been. *Don't you want to be a Pepper, too?*

Margreta von Pein

EMPTINESS

For three days I had not spoken. I was on vacation at a friend's house. It was mid-winter. There was no phone. There were no visitors.

Sometimes, I played her out-of-tune piano.

When I tired of reading, I fell asleep in her deep blue chair. Once, I slept all morning, after staying up all night to read a mystery novel about Tibet. I finished book after book without speaking to anyone.

My friend had left me an elaborately photographed text, a collection of testimonials by the devotees and disciples of the *guru.* The previous summer, I had visited her in the mountains to be blessed by her peacock feathers. She had glared angrily at me, as if I should not have sought an audience with her amongst all those Americans in *saris* and designer jeans.

I am old and unstylish.

Now, half a year after my meeting with the *guru,* the same face burns at me from the inert page.

The sun comes around the cold gray house and spreads its low light onto the snow-dusted hills. A dozen black-and-white cows pastured nearby loaf around a half-filled rick.

It is probably zero degrees outside. The cows' breath crystallizes in front of their faces. Heat fog hovers over their broad bodies as they lie down, one after another, for their morning chew.

Naturally, I become the cows. I am hot, digesting in sub-freezing cold. Bovine heat radiates through black-and-white winter fur. My mouth moves. I am literally ruminating. I am cows. Bent-kneed. Huge-haunched.

I am mindless. I am undifferentiated from the hay and the snowy, frozen ground.

The instant I recognize that I am cows, I am myself again. I am sitting in the blue chair in the morning sunlight and watching Holsteins in a pasture five hundred feet away.

I speak my first word in three days, "Mother."

Cathy Capozzoli

BEYOND RECOGNITION

To all of my daughters: I am one
who cannot name my grandmothers,
though Mother was my own.
I suffered her rock. Our family
still believes in heaven and hell,
even if birds don't sing
among leftover bricks. For us,
it's the knowing. With dinner,
we will address the holy land,
thirteen pails to water a single camel.
Candles and sage dry my mouth
like a cup held long to the sky.
Rain is part of the sun. Damp,
some would say, but hard red clay
forgives the long winds. What do I
owe you?

Marilyn S. Steele

LIFE IN THE ROUND

In the beginning was thought, and her name was Woman...She is the Old Woman Spider who weaves us together in a fabric of interconnection.

—Paula Gunn Allen, *The Sacred Hoop*

There are rows of rain clouds blossoming like white winter peonies along the horizon. Above them float two gray-winged clouds that look like eagle shadows. A string of raindrops hangs like pearls on a spiderweb. Each one is a glistening world of its own, and yet each one reflects every other jewel in that glittering lacework.

On the radio Claude Bolling and Yo-Yo Ma are playing a tune called "Baroque in Rhythm." The yearning of the cello seems to ask, *Do you, do you ever wonder why you're here?* The jazz piano dances alongside. Eventually, they move into a joyful ragtime.

There are so many levels of meaning, from Bach to boogie-woogie, weaving a rich tapestry of vibrations and rhythms and feelings. These are not visible but felt, like the gossamer web of relationship that connects us all.

We once knew our place in nature. We once approached the mystery of a world imagined as the Great Mother. Thousands of years away from the feminine principle, we became soul-sick and gravely harmed our beautiful planet. This morning's news tells of hundreds of seabirds—cormorants, grebes, and loons—that have been found dead along the California coast. Many of them are emaciated. There is less food in the ocean for the orcas and for us. We have forgotten what it means to be human, to be connected to wildness.

The ecological holocaust is twofold: It has to do with the gross overuse of our external environment, and the incredible underuse of our internal environment.

— Jean Houston

We must go down to the roots, to the mythic traditions where we all began. It is time to become a culture of dreamers. It is time to awaken to the ecology of self, to listen to the emergent wisdom of the dynamic, transformative feminine.

Twenty years ago Grandmother Spider Woman presented herself to me in a dream:

My youngest daughter, Azzia, is three years old. I take her outside to show her the beauties and joys of nature. We hold hands. We meander at the slow pace of wonder. We explore. We begin to pick things up from the ground — stones, a gracefully shaped twig, a burnt ochre leaf. Earthworms appear. She picks a fleshy one up to admire it. I try to be enthusiastic. The first worms that come up from the ground are ordinary brown-and-pinkish worms, but the next batch are spotted and striped in many different colors. Fascinated, we pick them up to examine their marvelous patterns.

A spider emerges from the ground — a plain, wiry daddy longlegs. The next spider is thicker and brown. It's a common household spider. A black spider with red dots and all kinds of colors and patterns follows. Then, a furry tarantula sidles over. I stifle a shudder, summon my courage, and let the spider crawl along my arm. Azzia isn't afraid. She is only curious.

A wondrous black spider comes strolling along. She is as huge as an ancient tortoise. Two cobalt-blue silk antennae stick up on either side of her head. They are almost transparent. They can turn to all sides to see, like periscopes. Behind these delicate antennae are large pink feathers. On her back are soft white plumes. She is a stunning and glorious creature!

Pausing for a moment, she heads purposefully down the dirt path that leads to the left into a dense forest. She expects us to follow. I do not hesitate.

As we leave, I see my father. He sits in a chair, off to the right, in the middle of a clearing. It is a place shorn of all living things. He is reading a book. "Father!" I call. "Look at this fantastic spider!" But he is engrossed in his book. By the time he looks up, she has passed by him, and we are following her into the forest.

The Father sits in his chair, above the Earth, separated and impenetrable like a Newtonian atom. There is an illusion of control, of order. If His identity depends on this perimeter, connection will feel like a threat. He avoids the chaos of wildness, of his own feelings, though it is out of chaos that new order emerges. In the clear-cut, barren emptiness, limited to a narrow intellect, there is not enough to green our souls.

Who was it calling me, calling us as mother and daughter, deep into the wilderness? What is the path into the forest?

We were called by the unknown, the mystery, the holy, and the numinous. The feminine way of knowing demands going into darkness, learning to live with chaos, finding the threads of meaning and pattern out of our own living. It is about opening to life, to the extravagant wealth of reality. We must learn how to stretch between opposites. We must bear the darkness and love the light. We can create a work of art, our lives, out of our own substance.

We need to reweave the broken web of our being. In doing so, we can remake the world. We can see ourselves from the Earth up, rather than the sky down. We understand that we are mostly empty space. We are more liquid than solid, and always becoming. We are the universe in person. We are of the Earth, not on it. We carry the ashes of stars in our bones. We look out through seawater. The spark of life that animates each of us was first lit at the dawn of creation.

The shift in our consciousness needs to be not only from a mechanistic view to a holistic one, but also from a timeless universe to an evolving and creative one. As part of a planetary web of consciousness, we can realize the noosphere that Teilhard de Chardin described. All minds are evolving together.

Joseph Campbell, at the end of his life, told us that we needed a new planetary mythology, one based on the crisis and conditions of our times. We have lived with a mythology of fragmentation for thousands of years. The most powerful and pervasive source of fragmentation is the identification of our individual selves as absolute, separate, and distinct from others. We now know that this is a mistaken and dangerous idea. It has fostered devastation, destruction, and despair throughout the world. By withdrawing from a sense of the sacred, we have poisoned the well waters of the land and the wellspring of our souls.

What's being lost is almost everything. One ant is no ant; one human is not human.

The problems of both psychology and ecology are worldview problems. "The transformation of our worldview necessitates the transformation of our view of the feminine," said James Hillman. When we reconnect to the dynamic, transformative feminine, we restore our connection to the natural world and also to our own souls.

Bringing indigenous intellectual and religious traditions together with the sacred feminine and new science, we can reimagine our world. There are new myths emerging to seed the future. There are new songs to sing it all into being.

The world of female integrity is a green world. We must honor the authority of wildness.

The time is now. Leading us is the wisdom of the grandmothers. They are appearing to us in various ways. Grandmother Spider Woman is the universe dreaming us into loving the beauty of the world. I think she has been telling stories to the physicists, who believe that we are vibrating strings interacting with each other. The universe is more like a symphony than a corporation of matter. As we learn about string theory, perhaps we can take in the picture of a universe that is not only like a web, but like a great stringed instrument, a dynamic vibrating instrument. We each have a song to play.

We vibrate in the energy waves of probabilities. They shimmer in the multiple dimensions of being, until an act of observation or engagement precipitates them into the particle nature of things. It is our responsibility to participate as co-creators. The Hawaiian word *kuleana* has an especially apt meaning of responsibility: Own your gifts, and share them with the world. It is especially time for the women to come forth. They are the ones we've been waiting for, as well as the men who understand and serve the sacred feminine.

It is no coincidence that creativity and the feminine come forth together. Creative individuals in this culture are called upon to abandon the masculine ground of collective consciousness and descend to the mother-realm in order to bring forth what demands to be born into the new age.

—Janet Dallett, "Artist, Analyst, Shaman, Thief," *Psychological Perspectives*, Vol. 17, No. 1, 1986

The old structures—economic, social, and political—are dissolving. We are at a bifurcation point where the system can either shift, leaping into a new pattern more inclusive and complex, or collapse into death. It is the new feminine archetype—the dynamic, transformative principle—that is leading the way. Eventually, after the old structures have dissolved, there will be a breakthrough to a new order, a new pattern that connects. We, the women, are the pilgrims and pioneers. We are the midwives and the mothers of this new emerging world. Ever unfolding, we are extravagant beings. We are as rich and complex as the world outside. When we truly understand the truth of our interconnection and the fragility of our shared web of life, we will have peace.

The basic ordering principle is kinship. Both the masculine and feminine principles are necessary. They are not polar opposites, but complementary.

There are signs of hope: Obama is in the White House. We note his attending to the memories of his mother and grandmother. We witness his care and respect for his wife and his daughters.

Maria Shriver, California's First Lady, is beginning an exciting new project called "A Women's Nation" to foster women's leadership. It is the women who best understand our interdependence. It is the women who know the urgency of protecting the Earth for our children and the next seven generations.

Revisioning. Reconceiving. Reconciling. Reinventing. There is a quickening from the depths of the Earth and from our own being. We are birthing a different understanding of what it is to be human.

We are guided by a creative process calling us into the future. This is the morphic resonance that Rupert Sheldrake describes. These are the archetypes of the collective unconscious.

Our brains are like tuning systems. We are tuned in to our collective memory and our collective becoming. We are not our past. We are not our present. We are always in the process of becoming, and we carry this process into being.

The journey to a wild feminine wisdom is a weaving way. it is a sometimes harrowing path, until we can become self-earthed, rooted in our natural feminine sourceground.

A different kind of world is possible.

Another world is not only possible, She is on her way. On a quiet day, I can hear her breathing.

— Arundhati Roy

I hear her breathing and singing. The universe hums. It quivers in tune. We are instruments for singing new heart songs, for bringing a new world into being.

Sing. Sing without stopping.

Linda Swanberg

BLESSING OF BEES

The linden tree ablaze—
bees sip on pale yellow blossoms,
move raggedly in drifts across the huge tree canopy.
Under the tree, sitting on a bench, I hear rustling in the sky,
a goddess shaking ribbons from her golden hair.
So many silk tassels teased by the wind,
I cannot begin to count.
Each spring the ritual is renewed: a few honeybees
in April crocus. A faint whir in creeping thyme.
Soon the whole garden will be buzzing.

On the porch at dusk, our voices low,
we speak about the day—soft murmuring
not unlike the bees.
We live in similar quiet fashion:
I care for our old collie's teeth, watch as you and I
move in and out of occasional sadness.
When limbs of older trees crack—break off in heavy winds—
we sigh; marvel at our new birch, 'Trost's Dwarf.'
Hum of buzzing illuminates who we are,
what we are about, how we will pass the days.
If we are appendages of this earthly body,
and our one great body wakes from a dream—
what are we to make of it, ourselves being a part of it?

For just as easily as we are born into beauty
(a bee finding nectar in abundance, the ecstasy of buzzing),
so may we quietly slip into dark.
A misguided step here,
a turn there, and we may lie
in some dark wash—the night heavy with pronouncement.

A June summer night. 2:00 a.m.
I sit under the linden tree in total darkness.

With the bees I have made a pact: "What you give, I accept.
I hold you close — my life resplendent
as your thousand wings."

Joel Wachman

Entanglement

There is a clock in the room. It is installed on the wall across from Ruby's bed. It hangs about two-thirds of the way up to the ceiling. The room also has a view of the river and the tangle of roads that hugs its edge. It is early spring. The trees are still mostly bald. A few tender chartreuse leaflings can be seen poking out of a branch here and there.

Later in the season, it will be harder to see the river and the roads. A mature canopy will have made the room more intimate. With the leaves gone now, the March daylight pushes into the room. The light offers promise.

The clock on the wall across from Ruby's bed holds my attention — an industrial clock, about ten inches in diameter with a white background and numbers printed in black around its circumference. The minute and second hands are long and elegant as a piano player's fingers. The hour hand is stubby and lazy.

This clock reminds me of the ones in elementary school classrooms, the ones I watched impatiently until classes ended at a clumsy ten-minutes-'til or twenty-five-minutes-past.

Those clocks were connected by some mysterious electromechanical force. They were synchronized from a command post next to the principal's office. I would watch the sweeping hand tick away the seconds. It sprang like a cat from one tick to the next.

Then, without any warning, the minute hand would begin to swing wildly around. The hour hand followed, brushing away the hours as fast as my pulse was racing. School's out. Dinner time. Homework. Bedtime. Night. Bus arrives. Math. English. Lunch.

Finally, the clock would stop its crazy ride. The hands would freeze just a few minutes before or after their origin. The second hand would begin its ticking again as if nothing had happened.

I half expect the clock across from Ruby's hospital bed to do the same thing. After a few hours of watching it, however,

I realize that the time doesn't matter. Time is a fickle measure of the events in our lives. We don't need a clock to prove this.

We arrived at 8:30 p.m. We had been at our favorite diner two hours earlier, when her water broke. Ruby was uncomfortable on the banquette. She kept reaching across her humpty-dumpty belly to get at the corned-beef hash. We chewed without talking.

Suddenly, she looked down at her lap and said, "I think I spilled my soup."

I pulled a bunch of napkins from the dispenser on the table and handed them to her.

Ruby looked up at me and laughed—a single elated, nervous *hah!* She hadn't ordered soup.

I helped her out of the banquette and walked her down the aisle.

We returned home to collect her things, feed the cat, and make the house tidy for our return. We pulled Ruby's overnight bag out of the closet, where it had been packed for weeks.

She took my hand. "When we come back, we'll be a family."

We knew how to be two together. What would it be like to be three? Even then, with Ruby's belly as large as it would ever be, with her skirt stained with amniotic fluid in the laundry basket, I did not believe that I was going to be a parent.

I have never liked infants, and I was afraid I would not love mine. Babies are an encumbrance. Couples with babies are messy, preoccupied, and annoying. I was afraid of what we would become, afraid that my relationship with my wife and my incipient child would not survive my unsuitability as a father.

Ruby should have taken her cue from the black widow spider by getting rid of me when she got pregnant. What a stupendous level of arrogance to think I had the capacity to care for a human being no larger than a bread box. I needed confidence, support, proof that I would not be an utter screw-up as a dad. Of course, proof never comes when you need it.

Images of our early relationship flashed through my mind. Our years in the Paris apartment. A train trip to Italy. Dinner parties. Long, quiet nights reading, lying on the sofa with our legs entwined.

As I stood there, I tried to send a message back to our earlier selves. *Enjoy it. It will not last.*

Ruby squeezed my hand. "I'm having a contraction," she said. "We should go."

We closed the door and began the drive to the hospital.

"It's a new chapter, you know," Ruby said.

• • •

Quantum entanglement is a phenomenon in which two subatomic particles appear to act as a single system. A change applied to one particle in an entangled pair is instantly manifested in the other, even if the two particles are separated by a great distance. Two photons, Alpha and Beta, traveling away from each other appear to be in cahoots about their polarities. Alpha encounters a pair of polarized sunglasses and goes through. Beta is stopped in his tracks. Alpha is influenced by a magnetic field. Beta changes his trajectory. The two particles are connected in a way which eludes explanation, though it is observable and repeatable.

We become entangled in our relationships—with our lovers, our siblings, our children. We know we are entangled when an unexplainable sense of urgency comes over us to pick up the phone, we call a dear friend, and the first words out of her mouth are, *Oh! I was just about to call you. Such-and-such a thing has happened to me.*

Twins are entangled when, in Baltimore and Seattle, they propose to their fiancées on the same day.

We think of these occurrences as mere coincidence, kismet, freak accidents. We laugh them off in the same manner that we dismiss ESP or communication with space aliens. (Our culture of science requires a phenomenon to be repeatable before it can be accepted as fact.)

Human entanglement may not be scientifically verifiable, but it does occur.

When do Baby and Ruby stop being one person and become two? When the umbilical cord is cut? When he pops out of her like a watermelon seed pressed between wet fingers? Or much,

much earlier, as a fetus, a zygote, a few-celled oocyte? This question is at the center of a heated moral debate. The question itself, though, is flawed. Mother and child are entangled from the moment the woman realizes that she is pregnant. They remain so even when the mother is seventy-five and the child feels guilty of not calling her.

• • •

The clock on the wall reads 9:20 p.m.

Outside, the traffic has slowed to a near halt. The river is adorned with a necklace of lights, red on one side, white on the other.

It has become harder to see past my own reflection in the window. I close the Venetian blinds with a clack.

Ruby, doped on Nubane, mutters, "Don't wake the baby." The baby is indeed asleep, curled up warm and safe inside Ruby's uterus, not ready to budge. Ruby's body is gently encouraging him outward and downward with brief contractions spaced three to four minutes apart. These tender hugs are nothing compared to the big squeeze that is to come.

The Nubane drip sings sweet lullabies to Ruby's insides. She is drowsy, cozy, and mildly hallucinatory.

There is not much in this room except the clock, the bed, a small linen closet full of swaddling blankets, and a stainless steel sink with duck-paddle faucet handles. They are the kind you operate with your wrists. On the wall opposite to Ruby's bed, a door opens onto a tiny antiseptic toilet. In the corner next to the head of the bed is a vinyl-cushioned chair. It reclines slightly.

I sit in the chair and tilt my head back to stare at the drop ceiling. The room is dark, and Ruby is snoring. There are seventy-five identical dark spots on each of the four ceiling tiles above my head. I begin to drift into my own version of a Nubane haze. My mind wanders. My head lolls back.

In the imagined future, Ruby, Ben, and I are eating pizza at the table. Ben pulls a piece of pepperoni off and eats it with his fingers. He is fastidious, at six years old. He wipes his hands on a napkin.

"Dad, which is bigger, a cell or an atom?" he asks.

"A cell is bigger."

"How many atoms could fit inside a cell?" he asks.

I want to tell him, but the number is too large even for adults to grasp. Ben, right on target with his psychological development, is incapable of conceiving of numbers more than a few multiples of his own age.

"A million million billion," I say, hoping that it sounds impressive.

"Are you still writing that science book?" he asks, with his mouth full.

I tell him that yes, it is taking a long time. I have been working on it since he was three. This causes him to raise his eyebrows in surprise.

"You write slowly," he says. "I wrote a twenty-five page book today."

"Oh, you did, did you?"

Ben taught himself to read and write before he left kindergarten. Now, at almost seven, instead of playing ball or riding his bicycle, he writes stories about his plush toys and their adventures on exotic Pacific islands.

"One minute. I'll go get it." He comes back from his room carrying a sheaf of paper stapled together into a book. The printing on the front is confident and clear: *The Uncertainty Principle*. It's a story about our Siamese cat Erwin, who is unable to decide whether to poop in his box or to poop outside. Most of the twenty-five pages are drawings of Erwin pooping.

One page of text reads, "He tries here. He tries there. Then he tries both places at once. Erwin is a special cat. He can poop inside and outside at the same time."

"That's a pretty profound book," I tell him. "Do you know what 'profound' means?"

"No," he says, "but did you read the dedication?"

On the back of the book he has written, "For my dad. Because he taught me to be a scientist."

• • •

Einstein did not believe in entanglement. He called it Spukhafte Fernwirkung — spooky action at a distance.

Quantum entanglement appears to break several serious laws of nature, not the least of which is that entangled particles can communicate faster than light. Physicists have rigged experiments to show that two entangled particles at great distances from each other will coordinate their states instantly. This challenges Einstein's theory of special relativity which claims light speed is an absolute limit of the universe. Not even the Starship Enterprise can travel faster.

Einstein's famous equation $E=MC^2$ shows that mass and energy are two aspects of the same thing, related to each other through the speed of light. Using this equation, we discover that pushing an ordinary object like a Toyota Prius to the speed of light would require enormous amounts of energy. It would require more energy than human beings have used since the discovery of fire.

If you could survive an experiment in which you sat in that car traveling at the speed of light, you would experience all manner of strange effects. Distances would become smaller. Time would slow down. In short, all of the natural ratios that we are accustomed to would start to flex and strain. You would enter a new world in which gravity, weight, distances, and time had unfamiliar relationships to each other.

Quantum entanglement, too, opens a can of metaphysical worms, forcing us to reorganize our understanding of the observable world, and our experiences of it.

• • •

The man who comes to give Ruby an epidural looks to be from the other side. His fingers are long, articulated fossils that clatter against the metal cart he pushes into the room. He speaks to Ruby with a whisper of cold breath. His lower lip trembles as if it were afraid of the rest of his face. This is a man who likes to take people to the brink. I surmise he ushers them back with reluctance.

Ruby has insisted on an epidural since the pregnancy test came back positive. She spoke of it with a tone of glad entitlement. She expressed *schadenfreude* for the generations of women who had labored before her with nothing more than a pan of hot water and a slug of whiskey.

"Natural childbirth," she quipped, "is when you arrive at the maternity ward without any makeup."

I do not begrudge her the right to mitigate her pain. The fact that science has found a way to selectively shut down her nervous system without hurting mother or child is admirable. Now that I have seen the face of the succubus that is going to administer the potion, however, I am filled with dread.

To make matters worse, Adele insists that I take a break. Ruby gives me a wink and a thumbs-up.

It is nearly 3 a.m., and I am aching for coffee. I relent. I follow the empty hallways toward the cafeteria on the first floor. I am accompanied only by the squeaking of my Hi-Tops.

I mumble, "What did they want to hide from me?"

Was there something horrible that would cause the squeamish to faint? Should I worry about an anesthesiologist who insists on working without witnesses?

The cafeteria is closed. Still, it smells of rehydrated eggs and bacon grease. A few vending machines stand at the end of the serving area, beyond the row of stainless-steel steam tables and lonely pastry cases.

The machine that sells hot drinks has an enticing sign. It depicts a steamy cup of fresh coffee. I know before I put the first quarter into the slot, however, that what I am about to receive will taste like diluted potting soil.

The dining area is empty except for a disheveled man with an unlit cigarette in his hand. I sit a few tables away from him. The cup of coffee doesn't taste like potting soil. It doesn't taste like anything at all. This is a good thing, because I calculate that I will have to consume at least two of them to raise my caffeine level to a useful concentration.

Above me are eighteen floors of sick people, recovering people, people giving birth, and people dying. It will be two more days before I can take my wife and newborn home.

My reflection in the window is dour and rumpled. I look almost twice my age. Maybe it's the cheap fluorescent lights.

When I stare into the glass, I see the face of my father. What would he say if he were here, instead of back at the retirement community and waiting for a joyous phone call?

He might say this:

"It's not going to be easy. In some ways it'll be harder for you than it was for me. Back in my day there were different expectations. I was just expected to do my job and support the family. I was not a 'new age man.' I never changed a diaper or did the middle of the night feedings.

Things are different now, but you're a natural. Love comes easy to you. At times, this has been your burden.

"When you moved to Europe, I thought it was the most selfish thing you could possibly do. I felt as if a part of me had been torn away—a limb or a vital organ. Like people who are missing a limb, I experienced a phantom. I could tell when you were happy and when you were lonely. When you fell in love, I knew it at once. When your heart was broken, I was troubled. A parent can feel this way about his children and still have his own inner life.

"Now that you're about to have your own child, everything will change. The center of your world will shift. Don't think the universe centers on him, though. It is somewhere between the three of you—you, Ruby, and this new little boy.

"Each of you will have your own life, but you will be entangled. It is a rare gift. Look around you, and see how many of these little universes fail to coalesce. Yours will be strong because of the person you are, because of the people Ruby and your son will be."

That's what my father might say.

My childhood was like this. It was unconditional love mixed with the smell of Chesterfields and Old Spice. I forgave my father long ago for his moods, his outbursts, and his bigotries, as I hope my child will forgive me for mine.

Despite the fact that most of my child's physical form comes from the pasta and cheese Ruby has eaten over the past ten months, I know the seeds of that form come from my own body. It is not so much the physical as the transcendental that we share — not the particle but the wave.

When I return to the hospital room, all of the lights are on. The welcoming, cozy atmosphere has been replaced by hot urgency. One nurse is at Ruby's bed. Another stands across the room, where she fiddles with a high-power standing lamp. The anesthesiologist has gone. Ruby is scowling.

Adele is saying, "You're going to feel the urge to push, but don't push yet. We're just getting you set up, honey, and you don't want to exhaust yourself."

Ruby takes my hand. "You missed the fun," she says. "They had to take the epidural out. The anesthesiologist screwed up, and I passed out. They had to revive me with some sort of antidote." Adele is putting the finishing touches on a saline drip in the back of Ruby's hand.

"He's not one of our favorites, that one," she says without looking up. The other nurse finishes her work with the spotlight and rolls it into position, where it will shine between Ruby's legs.

Ruby continues, "It was scary how completely I blacked out — and when I came back it was like climbing out of someplace dark and cold. I thought I had already had the baby. I mean, I really believed that it was all over.

"When I woke up a little more, I couldn't feel my legs. I didn't see any baby, and you weren't here. I was staring down the bed, and nobody was here. I was terrified. I thought I had died.

Baby is still crunched up inside her uterus. His head is pushing downward toward the birth canal. He is ready to leave the comfort and safety of the wet cave that has been his entire universe.

If I could pick him up and carry him away from the rude lights, from the heartless sterility of the hospital room, I would do so. I would spare Ruby the pain of giving birth. I would take her by the hand, our baby cradled in her arms, and walk away from this place.

There is, however, no avoiding the birth ordeal. Nature requires it. It is the wrath of a cranky God, whose eons of quiet solitude ended when the universe exploded out of nowhere, filling the infinite vacuum with heat and matter and a million needy voices crying out for help.

We, his creatures, bear his arbitrary indignities—a painful birth, a fleeting life dappled with suffering, an inevitable return to darkness. In our defense we form families and communities. Each time we bond with our parents, make a friend, take a lover, bear a child, we take solace in our severalness.

Even at our loneliest moments, we are not as isolated as I think God is. We will always be among others of our kind. This is what sets us apart from dark matter. It is the unified theory of human entanglements.

God will always be One.

The on-call obstetrician has arrived. She is an attractive woman with dreads. She wears hospital blues and eyeglasses. Her name tag simply reads, "Brice." She takes my hand—not so much to shake it as to hold it comfortingly—and tells me where to stand.

"Will you want to cut the umbilical cord?" she asks.

Cutting the cord seems too heavy with symbolism. Today is about joining the three of us as a family, not about encouraging my newborn's independence.

I struggle to decline without sounding squeamish. All I can manage is, "No, thanks."

She takes Ruby's hand, too, but not the same way. She puts Ruby's arm around her waist, as she sits on the bed. Brice knows that this is the way to gain Ruby's confidence.

"Now, Ruby," she says, "I can't say that this is going to be fun, but it's not going to be as horrible as you might think."

"Oh, really?" Ruby is eating it up. "Just how bad would you say it's going to be?"

"Worse than a bikini wax. Not as bad as breaking a leg."

"I can live with that," Ruby says.

Brice comes around to stand between Ruby's legs. "Just one

simple instruction. Push when I say, 'Push.' Don't push when I say, 'Don't push.' Okay?"

"Okay."

"Great," Brice says, putting her mask on. "Let's have a baby."

I would sound like the perfect man, if I could say with conviction that I felt Ruby's pain as she gave birth. (Is there a patron saint of laboring women? Is there a Native American story of a miracle worker who could steal women's pain and throw it into the river?) The fact is, I didn't feel a thing.

I tried the absurd thought experiments that women had told me would simulate the experience: Imagine pulling your upper lip over the top of your head. Men with foreskins, imagine something similar. Imagine passing a kidney stone the size of a billiard ball.

None of this imagining causes actual pain in my body. All it does is reinforce the fact that something is happening over there, in Ruby, that is not happening over here, inside me.

There have been moments when we have experienced the world with one mind—the view of the Piazza San Marco, or the pairing of a cheese from Rocamadour with a bottle of St. Emilion. Most of the time, however, our interior lives are inaccessible to one another.

At this moment we are definitely not entangled. All I can do is hold her hand and watch. She writhes and sweats and grunts.

I marvel at how far humanity has come, at how diligently we have applied ourselves to medicine and science and technology, and yet how in many respects we still resemble barnyard animals.

All at once there is light.

I think at first that it is an obscure flap of Ruby's insides, red and speckled with tiny hairs, but it is moving outward. Brice has her hands under it.

Then, it stops being part of Ruby and becomes its own thing, round and miniature. This is our son's head.

． ． ．

Buried in the Earth's crust beneath the Swiss-French border, the Large Hadron Collider is revving its engines. It is getting ready to blast tiny helpless Hadrons to smithereens.

The Large Hadron Collider is a seventeen-mile tunnel lined with lead and kitted out with enormous electromagnets. It is the largest and most expensive scientific apparatus on earth. When it is turned on, two beams of subatomic particles will chase each other around the circle at nearly the speed of light. The experiment itself will commence when the two beams collide somewhere on the clock face of the circular tunnel. (At noon? Quarter-past three? It doesn't matter, since time is eradicated at the point of collision.)

When two high-energy particles slam into each other, most of the energy will be turned into smaller particles. The more energy that is released, the more closely the experiment will approximate the conditions of the Big Bang.

With sufficient energy, colliders like this may one day validate a controversial idea that all of the subatomic forces are made from strands of energy called strings. Strings vibrate and undulate in unimaginably complicated ways. Strings reach across long distances and touch each other, quicker than the speed of light. Strings are smaller than any known subatomic particle, but they keep planets in their orbits and power the stars.

Even as we learn more about the origins of the universe, the answer recedes by another order of magnitude. We chase it down the infinitely small and infinitely deep rabbit hole, only to find there is another infinitely small and infinitely deep rabbit hole inside.

The evidence that comes of Big Science Experiments will reveal what the religious faithful have been saying for centuries. We are all bound together by a single unifying force that has numerous manifestations. Energy, time, gravity, and matter are all aspects of the same thing. God is One. We are created from

His raw materials, the raw materials being One. The One gives us form, substance, and duration.

If entangled particles behave like One, it is because they are bound together by this unifying force. Our own bodies and souls are wrinkles in this same fabric. Our lives are the result of a happy collision. Yes. We have free will and individual natures. At the same time, we are just like clay, made of molecules and atoms. The strings that make up those atoms bind us together.

The clock reads 5:30 a.m on March 11, 2000.

Ruby is in a deep sleep. Her face is the picture of abject relief.

Baby Ben is cradled in my hand. He is as small as a cat, and as quiet. The expression on his face is beatific. His eyes are wide open.

Though I know that he is neurologically incapable of seeing more than the shape of a nipple, I believe that he is looking at me, into me.

I stare into his eyes. I lose my balance. I fall into their translucent blueness.

I feel myself swept into a tight vortex prescribed by three points: Ruby is sleeping in the bed. Baby Ben is in my arms. He is looking up at me. My own face is staring down.

I am spinning like a quark. I am flying in circles through a magnetic field, rotating with the axis of the Earth. I am orbiting the sun in this Ferris-wheel tour of creation.

Marlene DeVere

WATER BURN

When my mother was four years old, she reached up to grab a teapot on the stove and pulled down a moment of terror. Boiling water poured along her inner arm and created an instantaneous burn.

Her grandmother heard her screams and ran into the kitchen. She ripped the forming scar off her arm, scooped her up, and dashed out of the house to the doctor's office, two blocks away.

"Nothing more needs to be done," the doctor said.

My mother's arm healed without a scar.

Her grandmother was about 40 at the time. Born in Palermo, Sicily, she died less than 65 years later in Chicago, Illinois. I only know her through my mother's memories.

According to family folklore, neighbors sought her out to mend their bodies, if not their souls, with her simple remedies. She was the poor person's doctor and priest, giving comfort with her healing touch.

My mother said that after her doctoring, she would say a prayer over the sick. She would anoint them with holy water, while making the sign of the cross on their foreheads. When she died, veins rose on her forehead in the form of a cross. She was buried that way.

• • •

A week before my mother died, my Aunt Mary came for a visit. She had been dead herself for nearly eight years. I had never dreamed of her until this time. The thing that surprised me about her visitation was how nice she was to me. This was a kinder, gentler Aunt Mary than I remembered.

I told my family about the dream. Everyone was astonished. It was unbelievable. A nice Aunt Mary? None of us could imagine that. I now believe that she was preparing us for my mother's death.

Reminiscing about Aunt Mary, we shared our favorite stories. My brother had the most outrageous one to share. He told of getting caught peeing on her living room drapes, when he was ten years old. He said he'd begged Aunt Mary not to tell Dad and, amazingly, she never did.

My story wasn't as inspiring. On my mother's thirty-third birthday, I wanted to do something really special for her. I recruited Aunt Mary for help. She reluctantly let me use her new electric eggbeater to make a cake in her kitchen. In no time flat, I had destroyed one of the blades. I still have no idea how I managed that.

Aunt Mary was pretty upset, and my mom had to pay for a new mixer. This was a catastrophic event for an eleven-year-old. My mom's celebration — and the cake — took a back burner to the broken eggbeater blade. In retrospect I should have peed in Aunt Mary's kitchen.

• • •

Mom worked for 45 years as a grocery store cashier. She was a whiz at basic math — able to add, subtract, multiply, and divide in her mind with such ease and efficiency that she was consistently the best employee in the store. She had to quit working when, after a series of strokes, nothing added up anymore. Toward the end of her life, when the dementia had taken away her ability to walk or speak and my father was unable to take care of her, she was moved to a hospice-type care facility.

When Mom was 81, a shower accident scalded her and left her with second and third-degree burns all over her emaciated body. Four weeks after being admitted to the hospital, she lapsed into a coma. My family was at her bedside, when the hospital chaplain administered the closest thing to last rites that she was sanctioned to do.

She explained that she was "like a priest." Because she was a woman, however, she could not be a priest. She could not give the Sacrament of the Sick to my dying mother.

I think my great-grandmother would have disagreed.

In the moments before she died, Mom smiled four times. Her eyes remained closed, yet her face appeared to be reaching toward something.

I like to imagine that she was seeing her grandmother, who, in those last moments, was scooping her up from her hospital bed and carrying her away from that misery to her new life. There, the water could never burn her again. It would be cool and refreshing. It would wash away her pain.

• • •

A week later, I stood on the beach alone. I carefully spread some of Mom's ashes. Their gray color was a stark contrast to the golden sand.

The tide retreated and took her ashes into the ocean. I cried and said the only prayer I knew by heart: "Please God, take care of her."

I stood there for a while. I hated to let her go into the unknown alone. I watched as the tide flowed back and forth.

As I turned to walk away, I saw something sticking out of the sand. Partially hiddden, it was enough to make me stop and take a closer look.

As I scratched the sand away, there were revealed two perfectly formed mollusk seashells. One was larger than the other. They were a mama and baby — coated in a lustrous mother-of-pearl skin.

The animals that had lived in the shells were long gone, but their legacy had survived. Whether the seashells came from Mother Earth or from my mother, they are a gift that I treasure. They are a reminder that nothing ever dies. It simply changes form.

Anne Higgins

THE ANGEL AND THE GARGOYLE

I'm into God. I perch on stone pillars,
spread golden light, and spew rain water.
I wear a halo. I wear bird dung.
I deliver messages. I spring and crouch.
Golden light is like honey. Dirt encrusts my cow face.
I accompany travelers. I guard the gates,
kneel over graves, and hunch over parapets.
I deliver death. I terrify children.
Wings are like hope, my brows like shelving.
I'm always eighteen; no one asks.
I sit with elbows on knees, palms raised in praise.
My eyes lift to heaven.

Anne Higgins

ANGRY ENOUGH TO DIE

God found Jonah and asked him, "Have you reason to be angry?"
    "I have reason to be angry," Jonah answered God,
    "Angry enough to die."

My shady gourd plant is gone,
my cucumber, my castor,
under which I found shelter,
within which I take heed.
Now I grope for the sky, that false mirror,
hot burning my skin —
Cancer blooms like a dandelion.
I have reason to be angry.

I have not tasted
the flavor of my tears.
Still, I mirror
Magritte's painting,
Flavor of Tears,
where the sand yellow leaf blooms as
a watchful hawk.
The leaf is the lace of his breast.
Grey sea gapes through it—

Angry enough to die.

I'll eat and drink
'til that sunset light
burns
clear through, I vow.

Still, He does not speak.

I lower my stony mask.
I listen.

B.E. Stock

FLYING IN THE SEA

One moment I seemed to drown.
Then strength arose from the deep.
Powerful lungs breathed ocean.
My body began to leap.
My arms divided the water.
My legs kicked currents aside,
as wrapped in a blissful shimmer,
I soared through the depths and cried.

With fear my joy was mingled
'til I thought my soul would crack,
for the one who flies into the sea
may not be welcomed back.

B.E. Stock

GOING OUT OF TOWN

I list a few things I will carry
and plan the departure time
and how I will fly to another zone
that is not where I am

My eyes grow unfocused and vague
for my heart is floating away
swollen with sweet sadness and fear
to the place where I will stay

I will send you no typical postcard
of ocean, hotel or lace
but rather a view of the round little world
taken from deep space.

Michael Lee Johnson

CHARLEY PLAYS A TUNE

Crippled
with arthritis and Alzheimer's,
in Chicago,
in a dark rented room,
Charley plays
melancholic melodies
on a dust-filled
harmonica he found
abandoned
on a playground of sand
years ago by a handful of children
who were playing on monkey bars.

Now, he goes to the bathroom on occasion.
Relieving himself takes forever; he feeds the cat when
he doesn't forget where the food is stashed at.
He hears bedlam when he buys fish at the local market
and the skeleton bones show through.
He lies on his back, riddled with pain—
pine cones fill his pillows and mattress.

Praying to Jesus and rubbing his rosary beads
Charley blows tunes out his
celestial instrument.
Notes float through the open window
and touch the nose of summer clouds.
Charley lets grief overtake him.
He is ecstatically alone.
Charley plays a solo tune.

Gabriella Tal

MY LAST GIFT

I speak from the heart of the one who has no voice left, the one who has not the ability to lift a limb, the one who can only express through the eyes. I speak for the one who appears to have no mind left.

Who knows what power directs the movements of my body or forms the odd words I speak? Trust that power. Trust the eyes. Trust the voice which can only touch one through silence or a sigh.

It is my last gift to you. I have given all I have now, and for my last offering, I give you all I can — the chance to serve.

I will give you little and sometimes no indication that I know or understand your offering. I may rebuff or hurt you without knowing. My anger may leak into our interactions. My pain may overwhelm you, so that you want to run, run, run away.

Run the way I cannot any more. Shake it out and dance it out the way I cannot any more. Shout it out the way I may not be able to any more.

You may want to turn from me. Then, you would miss the gift. The gift is in the vomit and the shit as well as in a piece of Mozart or jazz. The gift is in not getting back, in experiencing the sense of rejection that I may give. Look deeply into these words. Those who have lived it will understand what I say. Those who have not, take courage to dive into the paradox.

Sometimes, I do know what you are offering. Sometimes, I am very aware of it. Sometimes, though I cannot speak it, you will feel the murmur of my appreciation — appreciation which knows no bounds. In these last days, a clean bed is more important than gold. A kind word or a tender touch is worth mountains of diamonds.

If you turn from my gift, I will be all right. If I die without your help, I am cared for too. It is always that way, though it may not appear that way to me.

I may not have wisdom, but wisdom knows. Wisdom is my Master, and yours. Wisdom illuminates our days, our decisions, and our most necessary experiences. Wisdom shapes us like clay. Wisdom writes the scripts and directs them. Wisdom and kindness are sisters.

There is kindness in the most foul neglect, though one cannot fathom it from the perspective of the mind. Turn in upon yourself—ye that are cast away. Turn into the shell, the shell that holds you. The shell curls like a conch and wraps like love about you. You are home.

If the gift is received, it is good.

If the gift is not received, it is good, too.

It is my last gift to you. I have given all I have now. For my last offering, I give you the only thing I have left to give—the chance to serve.

Samuel Yanes

HIDDENBROOKE

The Stations of the Cross list the tasks,
Forwards and backwards,
A traveler's guide for the perplexed on
The Path of the Fall and the Path of Return.

It begins, or does it end
With a condemnation to death,
The bondage of *ahankara,*
For those who miss the opportunity within.

Can this judgement be reversed, and
Save his suffering Life?
He believes so and knows
With God, all things are possible.

So, laden with the true rood
Of cypress, cedar, palm and olive,
The spiritual man assumes his burden
At the crossroads of the Journey.

He falls for the first time, but not the last,
Going down, going down, going down
In *karmic* retribution,
A creditor coming to claim a big debt.

He sees his mother Mary standing before him,
Maia, mother of Hermes,
Maya, mother of Buddha,
But the hour is not yet come, and relief is near.

Simon, the Cyrenean, the Radiance,
Descending from the House of the Holy Spirit
Helps to bear the cross
In an act of spiritual love

And Veronica, wiping his face,
Purifying, cleansing,
Lightening the weight in his head
Lifts the higher faculties of his thought.

Falling again, he senses the second stage.
His consciousness focused on fire,
He sees the four beasts as
His soul is beckoned from above.

But even then he pauses and stops
To console the women of Jerusalem,
Paying attention to the House of the City
As he falls again for the third time.

Stripped of his garments and drenched with gall,
He tastes the bitterness of disillusion
As he is nailed to the cross,
Dilacerated like Osiris and Dionysus.

And when he dies, an Arrow of Light
Shoots out from the Heavens
Mortally wounding the darkness
And transfiguring the true man.

Free from bondage, he is taken from the cross,
And in his tomb
He awaits Resurrection and Redemption
And an outpouring of God's Grace

With profound dedication to the
Masters of Old and adoration of the
Divine Reality.

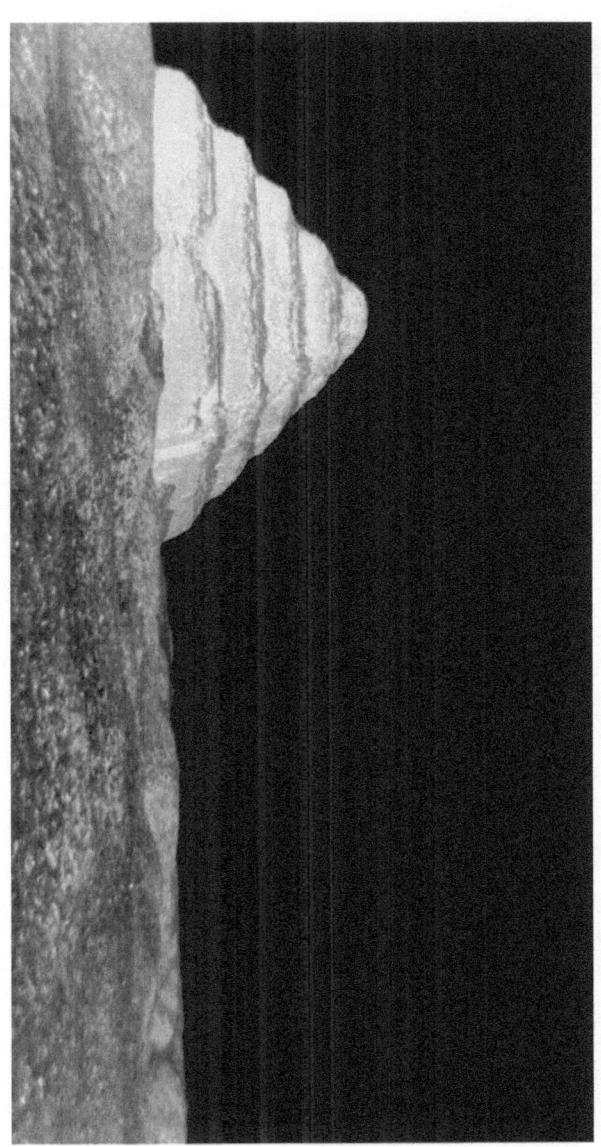

STEPPED PYRAMID

Michael Filimowicz

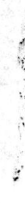

LIGHT WITH COLUMNS

Michael Filimowicz

Elisavietta Ritchie

CONUNDRUMS

to pick a chip
of ice from tiles
don't hold a second
in your fingers

some wisdom here
yet Chinese say
to catch a horse
must ride a horse

what if they both
gallop away
leave you dangling
from your saddle

you sprawl in frost
and slip on ice
your ride has fled
so in the end

not horse not ice
can be retrieved
you drink warm tea
then learn to walk

Elisavietta Ritchie

A CIRCLE OF STONES

alone on the beach
the print of one foot
did a man-bird
step once in the wet
of a briny pool
the tide kept
filling and draining
while everyone slept
beyond the sea's reach
the man-bird leapt
toes first in the foam
left a message drying
on fossil whale bones
he would not teach
but I overheard

Danusha Lameris

AT THE BAKERY IN CHINATOWN

At the bakery in Chinatown
we buy two cocktail buns,
still hot from the oven.

In the street, children light firecrackers,
toss them into sparse traffic.

What is this world—a bright sound
breaking in the road, or the sweetness
that we carry, still unopened?

Danusha Lameris

IT HAPPENED

It happened somewhere in snow country.
A boy slipped out the porch door
and wandered into the icy hills.
He was small — no more than three.
His parents, frantic, summoned help,
trudged into the wet woods.
Was he even wearing a jacket?
No one knew. Night came
and still, only the quiet
heaviness of the snow.
By morning, the answer:
He lay within a crèche of trees, asleep,
encircled by deer
who'd lain down, cloistering him
in their warmth. And now
when I think of grace, I think of this —
the boy waking in the night
to find, not his mother,
but the dreaming bodies of the deer
with wild fur, tails twitching, and damp noses
nestled between their hooves.

Barbara Wiedemann

MOUNTAINS AND PINE FORESTS

In the Idaho mountains near Silver City,
exposed rock
resembling the backs of dragons
marks the mountain ridges,
and on the steep slopes

purple stalks of lupine
Indian paintbrush
purple asters
and white and yellow of unknown others
struggle unaware.

Noticing all
but unnoticed
a woman hikes with a dog.

Lindsay Wilson

MEDITATION AT MOOSE CREEK

Today, when you cast your eyes out like a line,
     it's simply the light caught

on the surface of moving water, and,
     when your eyes lose focus,

the light becomes fish swimming
     toward the day's mild waterfall.

What you've always wanted is partly cloudy
     skies and a day in yellows. Tell us again

about salmon eggs, about the season
     in which the moon never rose. How did that

happen? How the sunlight stayed to fool you
     into thinking: fish on the fins of water.

Was it all a lure spinning out its light,
     which arrived late? Was it meant to conceal

a three-pronged hook of yellow flashes,
       bait and pull? And you bit, didn't you?

You bit when you tired of the difference between
       water and air. It's like that. You have to learn

not to bite a hook. You have to
       spend whole days trying to swallow the sun.

Lyn Lifshin

92 RAPPLE

I hardly remember which
window December's

moon fell thru
tho last light

hung behind tumbleweeds
and one maple tree

Someone said there was
a panther in the rhubarb

and trains sliced
ink nights. How little,

I thought, more than
had yet happened

would not blur
the longing for what

seemed only ordinary

Lyn Lifshin

HE SAID ONE MEMORY ON RAPPLE DRIVE

was the tumbleweeds
in the sandy back stretch.

I think, was it their
freedom, how

few roots they have
that we both think

of them? the sand
like a beach

he's finally close to
Rapple with "apple"

in it but more metallic
it's wall to wall

lush lawn, not torn up
he's still clutching the
DNA of cats old enough
to have a Ph.D.

if they weren't cats

K. J. Fraser

A Journey, a Reckoning and a Miracle: An Excerpt

George woke up with a headache. His wife was away, and there was no one else in the house, as it was Sunday. He felt stuck between the proverbial rock and a hard place. On the one hand, there were all the dreadful nightmares pressuring him to change. On the other, his closest advisors were demanding that he stay the course.

George still believed he would enter the history books as one of the founding fathers of newly formed democracies. He hoped it would happen in his lifetime, so he could walk the streets with adoring crowds throwing him flowers and candy.

"Ah, hell," he said to himself. Even he knew this was an unlikely fantasy.

George noticed his *Bible*, and his mood brightened. Religion had helped him before. Surely, God would help him again. He knelt and faced the bed. Glancing at the photos of his wife and daughters on the bureau, he prayed.

"Oh, Lord, I don't know what to do. Please help me."

He waited a long time with his head bowed, but the only sound he heard was the hum of the air conditioner. He began to wonder if perhaps he'd find God at church — maybe one he'd never been to before. He reached for the phone book on the nightstand.

Although he'd been to just about every church in a twenty-mile radius, he hadn't gone to any Catholic churches. Maybe he would find out something about that St. Therese of Lisieux.

As George got dressed, he marveled that St. Francis, who'd been born almost one thousand years ago, was still remembered and loved by people today. Machiavelli had been born about five hundred years ago, and lots of powerful people still admired him, too. George hoped people would remember him in a thousand years. Would they recall him as St. Francis or as Machiavelli? He shuddered to think he could be remembered as Machiavelli, or as another Hitler or Stalin.

The closest Catholic church was St. Eugene Church, just down the road in McGregor. The blurb in the *Yellow Pages* hadn't said anything about St. Therese but did mention Our Lady of San Juan and St. Philip. George didn't understand Catholics with all their saints, but those two sounded nice. Perhaps he'd ask the priest about St. Therese.

George was a bit surprised when he arrived to find himself at the Spanish-speaking service. Still, he knew some Spanish, and everyone looked friendly — though they didn't seem to recognize him. George thought this was wonderful, to be in a church without everyone fawning all over him.

"Thank you, Lord. I think you've answered my prayers this morning," he muttered.

He sat in a pew toward the back. This was, again, an experience he hadn't had in a long time. He was pushed to the front of every church he entered.

The Secret Service agents sat discreetly near the aisle, and a young mother in her Sunday best sat on the other side of him. She was accompanied by two young girls dressed in pretty frocks. Their long black hair was neatly tucked under flowered hair bands.

The girls had three paper fans between them. One of them offered the extra fan to George, which he graciously accepted. There was no air conditioning.

Opening up the fan, he saw a watercolor of a gentle-looking Mexican man, identified as San Juan de Lagos de Jalisco. Maybe they'd gotten these fans from a sister church.

George had difficulty deciphering the Spanish. It seemed to say that Juan was the saint most venerated in Jalisco, and that a similar saint had been sanctified and brought to the lower Rio Grande valley in Texas for the Mexicans who lived there. Expecting more about saints, he flipped over the fan — and almost dropped it, shocked by what the drawing depicted. It was a picture of a church with a plane crashed through the roof. George looked anxiously at the ceiling.

As the service started, he read the miraculous true story, written in English, of the plane crash. Close to eight hundred people, many of them children, had been sitting in the Hidalgo county church on Sunday, October 23, 1970, when a small plane inexplicably crashed through the roof.

Small churches are built as economically as possible. With the poverty of the lower Rio Grande Valley, their church had been built with great frugality. It must also have been built with great love and faith, because the plane had hit the one rock-solid steel beam in the roof. No one had been killed or even hurt. The statue of la Virgen de San Juan was unscathed. The story didn't recount what happened to the pilot.

George thought back to when those other planes had crashed into the buildings. He wished there'd been a steel beam of love and faith strong enough to prevent all those deaths. Sweating and trembling, he began to weep. He had mourned all those deaths, but there hadn't been time to really feel their loss, and now he was struck with the enormity of it.

He recalled the photos in the *Times* and the short bios that Laura had diligently read, even though neither of them usually looked at that newspaper. She'd said that it was a gesture of respect to read about these people, just as the *Times* had shown its respect by writing about them.

The priest droned on in Spanish, and George looked around for something to distract him. Along with saints, there were huge photos of young men and women in uniforms on the walls. He was glad to see their photos. Then, he noticed that each of the pictures was rimmed in black and had dates printed beneath them. The dates began with 1983 and 1979, and even 1991. They ended with 2004, 2007, and 2009. 2009. This very year someone's son had died in the service.

Sweat rolled down George's neck and shirt and stuck to his back. He looked at his hands. They had signed the death warrants for all these young people. His nose dripped. It seemed that he'd never felt so hot.

Perhaps it had been an enormous mistake to attend this church. He wanted to flee.

The young mother next to George passed him a lace-edged hanky, and one of the little girls gave him a piece of candy. He accepted both, cleared his throat, whispered "Gracias," and mopped his face. The priest had been talking in Spanish. Now, he switched to English.

Was it because he'd seen George's distress, or was this a part of the service? Either way, George would remember his words for the rest of his life. Luke 15:11-32.

The priest paused and looked out over the audience.

In fact, he knew who George was. He had voted for him the first time, but not the second. He had agreed with the Vatican, that the war was deeply immoral. Earlier this week, he'd been inspired to choose this famous passage from Luke. Now, he knew why.

"You all remember the story of the Prodigal Son. The extravagant son. Remember, prodigal means extravagant, although we think the word means lost. We have talked about this man many times before. He is the son who was given everything but left home and squandered his fortune. He became a swineherd, the lowest of the low at that time, as pork was not eaten by Jews. Meanwhile, an elder son had stayed home to care for his father, and had used his inheritance wisely.

"Many years later, the younger son realized his mistakes. He decided to return home and ask for forgiveness. Without any hesitation, the father gave his forgiveness and killed a fatted calf in honor of the youngest son.

"The elder son complained bitterly that he should have been given this great honor. He had stayed and done everything the father had asked.

"The father told him, 'Your brother was dead, and is alive again. He was lost and is now found.'"

The priest paused and remembered where he'd truly understood this story. It had been in a halfway house, where he'd ministered and seen true healing between people who'd been bitterly estranged for years.

"Just as the father forgave his son, so Jesus forgives those who make mistakes. He forgives the extravagant. He forgives the wasteful. He forgives the squanderers. He forgives and invites the prodigals to his table. Everyone is welcome at Jesus' table. Let us pray."

Everyone moved to their knees and bowed their heads.

As the priest said the Lord's Prayer, George, now on his knees, thought about the Prodigal Son. Wasteful. Extravagant. Squanderer.

He'd accepted Jesus into his heart years ago, but he wondered now if Jesus had accepted him. Seeing himself as the Prodigal Son, he began to pray for forgiveness.

It seemed like hours had passed before George sat back in his seat and heard the next words of the priest.

"Let us remember the dear soul of St. Therese of Lisieux, the Little Flower. Her motto was, 'Love is repaid by love alone.' She told us that it doesn't matter what position a person has in this life. It's the place you've been given by God. Everyone can find his or her place. It's never too late. Let us pray."

George had stopped crying. Time seemed suspended. He felt the awesome and gentle power of Jesus and St. Therese. Humility washed over him, as it had years ago when he'd quit drinking. He felt the same sense of grace. Yes, amazing grace.

"Thank you, Lord. Thank you, St. Therese."

He had found God through the *Yellow Pages*.

CONTRIBUTORS

EDWARD BLACK lives in Japan and Louisiana, where he teaches at Grambling State University, an historically black college. His stories have appeared in the *Tulane Review, Weber Studies, Apalachee Review, Jabberwocky Review, Reed Magazine,* and *Yomimono.*

ROGER CAMP has had images published in over 100 magazines including *Darkroom Photography, American Photo, New England Review, Photo Metro, Antioch Review, North American Review, NY Quarterly,* and the *Chicago Review.* He is the author of three books of photography: *Butterflies in Flight* (Thames & Hudson, 2002) *500 Flowers* (Dewi Lewis Media, 2005) and *Heat* (Charta/DAP, 2009). He has taught photography at the University of Iowa, Columbus College of Art & Design, and the Cité Internationale Universitaire de Paris. His awards include the Leica Medal of Excellence in documentary photography and Visual Fellow at the Fine Arts Work Center, Provincetown. His images are represented by the Robin Rice Gallery, NYC.

CATHY CAPOZZOLI was the guest editor of *Many Mountains Moving: The Literature of Spirituality* in 2002. This collection of creative works includes 88 writers and artists from six countries and spans many spiritual traditions. Her work has recently appeared in the *Griffin, New Millenium Writings, Evansville Review, Owen Wister Review,* the *Binnacle, Carquinez Poetry Review, Lake Effect, Tin Fish, Karamu, Mudfish, RiverSedge, Oregon East, Rock & Sling,* and *Hawai'i Review.* She holds an M.A. from Naropa University.

CHRISTOPHER CONNOLLY is a writer and therapist, who currently resides in the rural American West. He is endeavoring to create an organic farm and holistic health clinic. He is also establishing a literary press that will be dedicated to publishing the work of contemporary American poets. Continuing his resurgence from a period of debilitating illness, he encourages us to embrace life as an ever-evolving journey of new beginnings.

BRIAN CRONWALL teaches English at Kaua'i Community College in Hawai'i. His poems have appeared in numerous journals and anthologies in the United States, Australia, Japan, the United Kingdom, and France.

KEVIN DEHAN has had two plays performed in BlueBox Productions' Evening of Sticky on Manhattan's Lower East Side. It's no surprise that he finds himself now gravitating toward writing short stories, as they have always been his favorite form of fiction.

MARLENE DEVERE is retired from a career in teaching, broadcast journalism, and advertising. A native Chicagoan, she has lived in most sections of the country and in the Middle East. She is now living in Tucson, Arizona, and working on a collection of short stories.

ROD FARMER has had 850 poems published in 150 journals, including the *Kerf, Rattle*, and *Main Street Rag*. His most recent collection is *Red Ships* (Finishing Line Press, 2002).

MICHAEL FILIMOWICZ is an interdisciplinary artist and American Midwest transplant. He is based in Vancouver, British Columbia, where he teaches at Simon Fraser University. He works in the areas of digital photography, experimental video, sound design, public art, interactive new media, and creative writing.

BARBARA FLECK-PALADINO has published essays in the *New York Times*, *JAMA*, *Parents* magazine, and several small journals. These days, she most often shares her efforts with fellow members of a treasured writing group headed by Carol Emshwiller. Formerly a public school teacher of early-childhood classes, Fleck-Paladino is the mother of three adult sons, Louie Fleck, Bela Fleck, and Sascha Paladino. She lives on the Upper West Side of Manhattan with her husband, Joe Paladino.

HUGH FOX, originally from Chicago, got his Ph.D. in American Literature from the University of Illinois. He taught American literature, writing, and film at Loyola University in Los Angeles. He has also taught at the Instituto Pedagógico in Caracas, the University of Hermosillo in Mexico, and the University of Santa Catarina in Brazil. He has published 110 books. His latest is *The Collected Poetry of Hugh Fox* (World Audience, 2008).

FREDERIC FRANKEL, originally from South Africa, earned his advanced degree in psychiatry from the University of the Witwatersrand in Johannesburg, before migrating to the U.S. in 1962. He has been on the faculty of Harvard Medical School since 1969 and Professor Emeritus of psychiatry since 1997. He served as Psychiatrist-in-Chief at Beth Israel Hospital Boston from 1986 to 1997. Now retired, he attends poetry classes at the Harvard Extension School and studies with Barbara Helfgott Hyett. He is the author of *Hottentot Venus* (Pudding House Publications, 2003) and *In A Stone's Hollow* (Fairweather, 2006). He was awarded the Robert Penn Warren First Award of New England Writers in 2003. His work has appeared or is forthcoming in such publications as *Cape Codder, Concho River Review, Ibbetson Street, Jewish Currents*, the *Larcom Review, Moment, Passager, Ship of Fools*, the *Tusculum Review*, and in the anthologies *The Mercy of Tides* (Salt Marsh Pottery Press, 2003), *Rough Places Plain* (Salt Marsh Pottery Press, 2005), and *The Anthology of New England Writers* (New England Writers, 2003).

K. J. FRASER is a psychiatrist and person of faith who lives with her family in Albuquerque, New Mexico. Her first novel, *A Journey, a Reckoning and a Miracle* (O books, 2009), was inspired by the Iraq War, the 2004 election, and a former American president's avowed religious beliefs. For more information, please visit her website at www.jrmstory.com.

FRANKLIN GILLETTE is a Colorado native, now living in the Bronx. He won the '98 Starr Symposium poetry contest. He has been published in *Poetry East, Aurorean,* and other magazines. He is also a librettist, painter, *yoga* teacher and healer.

KATHIE GIORGIO has published stories in *Harpur Palate, Fiction International, Dos Passos Review, Ars Medica, Thema, Jabberwock Review, Karamu Review, Reed* magazine, *Bellowing Ark,* and others. Her writings have also appeared in the premier issue of *SLAB,* the premier issue of *Broken Bridge Review,* and in an online and audio anthology published by Susurrus Press and titled, *I Am This Meat.* She has been featured in *Women Writers'* e-zine. She has also appeared in anthologies published by *Main Street Rag,* among others. Her writings have been nominated for the Million Writer Award and the *Best of the Net* anthology. She is the director and founder of All Writers' Workplace & Workshop, a creative writing studio, and is the editor, owner, and publisher of *Quality Fiction* magazine. She teaches for *Writers' Digest* and serves on their advisory board.

KATHLEEN GUNTON lives in Orange, CA. While working on a memoir of her convent days, she continues to publish prose, poetry, and photography. Recent work has appeared in the *Christian Science Monitor, Blood and Thunder, Inkwell, Westview, NCR,* and *Thema.* She believes that one art feeds another.

RAYMOND HAMMOND is a poet and critic who, originally from Virginia, now resides in Brooklyn. He works at the Statue of Liberty as a law enforcement officer for half of the week and as Editor-in-Chief of the *New York Quarterly* for the other half. He holds an M.A. from New York University, where most of his classes were intense studies of poetics with William Packard over a hamburger at the Chelsea Gallery Diner.

ANNE HIGGINS teaches English and theology at Mount Saint Mary's University in Emmitsburg, Maryland. She has had 70 poems published in *Yankee, Commonweal, Spirituality and Health,* the *Melic Review,* the *Centrifugal Eye,* and a variety of small magazines. Her books include *At the Year's Elbow* (Mellen Poetry Press, 2000; Wipf and Stock, 2006), *Scattered Showers in a Clear Sky* (Plain View Press, 2007), and *Pick It Up and Read* (Finishing Line Press, 2008).

MICHAEL LEE JOHNSON is a freelancer from Itasca, Illinois. He has been published in more than 20 countries and edits four poetry sites found at www.poetryman.mysite.com.

RACHEL KANN has received accolades from the James Kirkwood Fiction Awards, *Writer's Digest* Short Short Story Awards, and *LA Weekly* Awards. Her work appears or is forthcoming in *Eclipse, Permafrost, Word Warriors,* and from Seal Press, among others. Rachel is the resident poet for daKAH, a seventy-piece Hip Hop Orchestra. She has presented her poetry in venues including the Disney Concert Hall, the San Francisco Palace of Fine Arts, and the Vans Warped Tour. She teaches poetry and fiction for the UCLA Extension Writers' Program. Rachel is also a budding DJ, an award-winning performance artist, and a mixed-media collage artist.

REVEREND JAMES "K" KARPEN serves as the pastor of the Church of St. Paul and St. Andrew in New York City.

DANIEL LADINSKY is one of the most successful poets writing in the world today. Known initially for his unique renderings of the fourteenth century Persian mystic, Hafiz, Daniel is now also internationally recognized for his gifted, deeply accessible renderings of Eastern and Western mystics. Daniel's four books, *I Heard God Laughing, The Subject Tonight Is Love, The Gift,* and *Love Poems from God,* are currently published by Penguin Books USA. They remain consistent top sellers in the genre of religious and spiritual poetry and show the marks of becoming enduring classics. His latest books are *A Year with Hafiz: Daily Contemplations* (Penguin, 2010) and *The Purity of Desire: 100 Poems of Rumi* (Penguin, 2010).

LALITAMBIKA is a poet, translator, and meditation teacher.

DANUSHA LAMERIS has had writings published in various journals and anthologies, including the *Crab Orchard Review, Atlanta Review*, the *Alaska Quarterly Review*, and *Lyric.*

LYN LIFSHIN has edited four anthologies of women's literature and has published more than 125 books, most recently *Barbaro: Beyond Brokenness* (Texas Review Press, 2009) and *Persephone* (Red Hen Press, 2008). She is the subject of a documentary film, *Lyn Lifshin: Not Made of Glass*.

LOKANATH (MIKE MAGEE) works as a British journalist. He has been close to the *shakta* tradition for more than thirty years. His site, www.shivashakti.com, reveals the depth of practice within the different Hindu tantric traditions.

SUMALEE MAHANARONGCHAI is Chair of the Graduate Program in Buddhist Studies at Thammasat University in Thailand. She is also a guest lecturer at Mahachulalongkorn Buddhist University, Rangsit University, and others. She is the author of 11 books, including *Mahāyāna Buddhism* (Bangkok, Siam, 2003), *Hinduism and Buddhism: Differerent Standpoints (Mahāyāna Perspective)* (Bangkok, Sukhapjai, 2003), *The Five Jina Buddhas* (Bangkok, Thai-Tibetan Centre, 2004), and *Nāgārjuna and His Teachings to The Middle Way* (Bangkok, Siam, 2005).

JAMES MARKAY is a meditator and a poet. He quotes Louise Gluck as saying, "My precept in consciousness is the fact that you cannot love what you refuse to know."

RICHARD MARRANCA regularly publishes essays, fiction, and poetry. His new collection of essays is *Dragon Cafe* (Bangkok Books, 2011). He has received a Fulbright to teach at the University of Munich, as well as five National Endowment for the Humanities summer study grants. Richard enjoys hiking, running, *yoga*, meditation, travel, and many other things. He lives in New Jersey.

BOBBY MINKOFF, PH.D. is a licensed psychologist in private practice and a professor of psychology and human services. He is also a storyteller. He is a member of the National Storyteller's Association.

MIREK is a devotee of Meher Baba.

GREG MOGLIA is a veteran of 27 years as an adjunct professor of Philosophy of Education at NYU and 37 years as a high school teacher of physics and psychology. His poems have been published in over 100 journals internationally, as well as five anthologies. He is five times a winner of the Allan Ginsberg Poetry Award sponsored by the Poetry Center at Passaic County Community College. His poem "Why Do Lovers Whisper?" was nominated for a Pushcart Prize in 2005. He lives in Huntington, New York.

AYAZ DARYL NIELSEN is a poet, husband, father, veteran, and hospice nurse. His poetry has found many homes worldwide, including *Hazmat, Lilliput Review, Magnapoets,* and *Shemom.* He is the editor and custodian of *bear creek haiku.*

MARGRETA VON PEIN lives in the San Francisco Bay area. She has had three short stories published.

MICHELE HEATHER POLLOCK is a poet and mixed-media artist who lives and works in the woods of southern Indiana. She is the author of two chapbooks of poetry, *Regarding Memory* (Cross Keys Press, 2002) and *A Clean Escape into Something Else* (Sarasota Poetry Theatre Press, 2003). Her work has appeared most recently in *Poetry East,* the *Dos Passos Review,* and *Broken Bridge Review.*

ELISAVIETTA RITCHIE is the author of 15 books and chapbooks. Her collections of poetry include *Arc of the Storm* (Signal Books, 1998), *Elegy for the Other Woman* (Signal Books, 1996), *Tightening the Circle Over Eel Country* (Acropolis Books, 1974), *Raking the Snow* (Washington Writers Publishing House, 1982), and *Spirit of the Walrus* (Bright Hill Press, 2005). Her fiction books include *In Haste I Write You This Note* (Washington Writers Publishing House, 2000) and others. Ritchie's work is widely published, translated, and anthologized. She writes, teaches, mentors, edits, translates, photographs, and serves as poet-in-the-schools.

MORGAN RUST is new to the art market, but has been creating artworks since early childhood. She believes that if all cultures would merge their strong points together as one, then paradise would come to planet earth—not by mixing peoples together like different colored paints, but by piecing them together to form a richly diverse mosaic of humanity.

SUSANNE VON SCHROEDER was born and grew up in southern Germany. She is the daughter of a Lutheran minister. As a teenager, explorations into the deeper meaning of life led her to join an overseas *ashram*. In 1987 she transferred to an *ashram* in the United States, where she was able to focus her attention on growing plants, eventually becoming the head grower of a large greenhouse complex. In 1999, she established her own flower gardens and nursery. This inspired her passion for nature photography. Meanwhile, reading the poetry of mystics such as Rumi and Hafiz has enabled her to explore deeper dimensions within her work. She says that looking through a camera lens changes her view of the world; macro photography allows her to see and unveil the hidden beauty surrounding us. Her photographs have been shown at numerous locations throughout the Midwest. She has published two photography books: *Seeing Beauty: Photography As Visual Poetry* and *Allow What Is* are available at www.blurb.com.

MAHESHWAR N. SINHA is widely published in the Hindi language, as well as in English. He is the author of the novelette *Tales of Mr. Dhenchu-Panchu* (AEG New York, 2008). He is also interested in painting, sculpture, sports, *yoga*, and medicine. He works as a government excise inspector in Jagdalpur, Chhattisgarh, India.

JOANNA SIT has taught literature and creative writing at Brooklyn College and NYU. She now teaches composition at Medgar Evers College. Her work has appeared recently in the *Tonopah Review*, the *Relief Journal*, *Natural Bridge*, *Fickle Muses*, and *Poem*. Her poetry appears in the anthology *Monologues From the Road* (Heinemann Press, 1999). Her translation of "Cause and

Effect" appears in *Seneca Review*, December 2008. She has read at the Knitting Factory, Teachers and Writers Collaborative, Dixon Place, La Mama La Galleria, the 11th Street Bar, KGB, and other venues in New York City.

ASKOLD SKALSKY, born in the Ukraine, teaches English at a community college in Western Maryland. He has had poems accepted by numerous small press magazines and journals, most recently in *Freshwater* and *Freefall*. He has also been published in Canada, England, and Ireland. Two years ago he received an award from the Maryland Arts Council for his poetry.

MARILYN STEELE, PH.D., a Jungian psychologist practicing in Berkeley, California, has taught widely in the United States and abroad on the psychology of women, the archetype of the dynamic, the transformative feminine, the evolution of consciousness, and a revisioning of the self. Her writing focuses on the wisdom and power of dreams to awaken our souls, and to heal ourselves and the world. Dr. Steele has published articles in *Family Therapy Newsletter*. A book review and poetry have appeared in the Jungian journal *Psychological Perspectives*. Her poems also appeared in the Madrone Avenue Press anthologies in 2005 and 2007. New work is forthcoming in *Zone 3*.

HELENA STEINER-HORNSTEYN is the author of *Constant Awakening* (Activale Books, 2007), *Who am I? and Where Am I Going?* (aMuse Productions, 2008), and others. She offers her spiritual gifts to help the world. www.activale.com

B. E. STOCK holds a B.A. in creative writing from Sarah Lawrence College. She was a contributor at Bread Loaf Writers' Conference in 1970 and 1971, and has studied under E. L. Doctorow, Jane Cooper, Muriel Rukeyser, Maxine Kumin, and Miller Williams. Her work has been widely published in magazines such as *Salt, New Press, Karamu, Wings, Array, Footwork, Spring, Piedmont Review*, and others. She has performed frequently in New York cafés and clubs, and has been a featured reader at the New York Poetry Forum, the Belanthi Gallery, the Shelley Society,

Borders, Shakespeare's Sister, The Old Stone House, and the
Fall Café, among others. She was a leading reader at the e.e.
cummings centennial reading at the Jefferson Market Library
in New York City in 1992.

DANIEL STOLAR is the author of a collection of short stories,
The Middle of the Night (Picador, 2003). His fiction and creative
nonfiction have appeared in a number of publications including
Bomb, DoubleTake, the *Utne Reader*, the *Virginia Quarterly Review*,
the *St. Louis Post Dispatch*, and the *Chicago Tribune*. He teaches
at DePaul University in Chicago, where he lives with his wife,
Lauren, and their two daughters, Callie and Anna.

LINDA SWANBERG of Missoula, Montana, received her M.A.
from the University of Montana in the 1970's. Since 2003, she
has studied with Tobin Simon, Director of the Proprioceptive
Writing Center. Her work has appeared in the *South Carolina
Review*, the *Cape Rock, Carquinez Poetry Review, Owen Wister
Review, CQ (California Quarterly), HeartLodge, Aries*, and others.
Swanberg lives with her husband Gregg and collie Chanel. She
is a musician. Tending a woodland garden has been her main
focus for the last twenty-seven years.

GABRIELLA TAL has been a lover of Meher Baba (knowingly)
for twenty years. She lives in Chapel Hill, North Carolina and
makes numerous trips to her Beloved's home in Ahmednagar,
India. A therapist and musician, she has written music to many
of Bhau Kalchuri's *ghazals*. Her greatest joy is to sing for him.
Her CD *Happiness Is Better* (2004), produced at Bhau's direction,
contains 20 of his *ghazals* sung by herself and other Baba lovers.
www.gabriellatal.com

JOEL WACHMAN is a writer and computer technologist. He has
written for the *Harvard Review* and the *Boston Globe*, and has
won awards for his works of creative nonfiction. He lives with
and derives inspiration from his wife and son in Cambridge,
Massachusetts.

BARBARA WIEDEMANN is a professor of English at Auburn University, Montgomery. She is also the author of a critical study entitled *Josephine Herbst's Short Fiction: A Window to Her Life and Times* (Susquehanna University Press, 1998). Her poems have appeared in *Kaleidoscope, Blueline, Kerf, Feminist Studies, Paper Street, Acorn*, and other journals. In 2008 her chapbook, *Half-Life of Love*, was published by Finishing Line Press.

LINDSAY WILSON teaches at a college in Reno, Nevada and edits the *Meadow*, a literary magazine. He is the author of four chapbooks and was a finalist for the Philip Levine Prize. His poetry has appeared, or is forthcoming, in the *Portland Review, Gulf Stream*, the *Blue Mesa Review, Talking River*, and the *South Dakota Review*, among others.

SAM YANES is a strategic communications consultant to numerous profit and not-for-profit institutions. His clients have included Prudential Financial Services, Merganser Capital Management, Intel Corporation, the Radcliffe Public Policy Program, Harvard University, the Smithsonian Institution, the Calderwood Writing Initiative at the Boston Athenaeum, the Garden Conservancy, and the Orentreich Foundation for the Advancement of Science. He worked for many years as Vice President of Corporate Communications for Polaroid Corporation, as an adjunct professor at the Graduate School of Communications Management at Simmons College, and as Deputy Director of the Jewish Museum. He was the founding editor of Big Rock Candy Mountain, the educational counterpart to the Whole Earth Catalog, and has authored three books on education and American lifestyles. Yanes has also served as President of the Board of the Institute of Contemporary Art, Boston; Commissioner of the National Museum of American Art, Smithsonian Institution; a member of the Board of Fellows of the Center for Creative Photography, University of Arizona; an Overseer of the Isabella Stewart Gardner Museum; President of the Beacon Cultural Foundation; a Director of Grantmakers in the Arts; and a member of the Advisory Board for Journalism at Brandeis University.

SUBSCRIBE

P.O. Box; 131 Planetarium Station; New York, NY 10024

____$10 One-year subscribtion (one issue)

____$19 Two-year subscription (two issues)

> Please add $4.95 for postage and handling and enclose a check written to *Lalitamba*.

Begin my subscription with issue number ____

Name_____

Address_____

City, State, Zip_____

Please send a gift subscription to:

Name_____

Address_____

City, State, Zip_____

SUPPORT SARANAM

Lalitamba is in partnership with Lalitamba Saranam, a women's shelter in New York City. Through years of working with people in need of permanent housing, we understand how stressful the situation can be. We offer the comforts of home to women in transition. ***To make a tax-deductible donation, please send a check to Lalitamba Saranam at the above address.*** Your generosity makes it all possible. Thank you! **www.threejewelsrefuge.org**

A Working Writer's
Daily Planner *2011*
Your Year in Writing

Packed with helpful hints, awards, grants, residencies, market listings, writing prompts, and more, this all-in-one planner is an indispensable tool to help writers stay on top of the business end of writing and encouraging them to keep at the business of writing itself.

'89350676 · Spiral bound · 6 x 9 · 160 pp · $13.95 · also available as a DRM-free ebook
ll color · class/group discounts available · Distributed to the trade by Consortium.

www.smallbeerpress.com · facebook.com/smallbeerpress

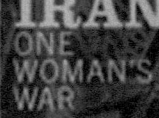